D0056203

MECHANICS' INSTITUTE
MECHANICS'
MERCANTILE LIBRARY

# THE LONG GOODBYE

# THE LONG GOODBYE

*Patti Davis*

ALFRED A. KNOPF   NEW YORK 2004

THIS IS A BORZOI BOOK
PUBLISHED BY ALFRED A. KNOPF, INC.

Copyright © 2004 by Patti Davis

www.aaknopf.com

Library of Congress Cataloging-in-Publication Data
Davis, Patti.
The long goodbye / by Patti Davis.
p.    cm.
ISBN 0-679-45092-0
1. Reagan, Ronald.   2. Presidents—United States—
Family relationships.   3. Davis, Patti.   4. Reagan,
Ronald—Health.   5. Alzheimer's disease—Patients—
United States—Biography.   I. Title.
E877.2.D38   1997
973.927'092—dc21      97-2994
[B]    CIP

Manufactured in the United States of America

First Edition

Thank you to Victoria Wilson for her insight and
wisdom, and for her patience in the long birth of this
book. To my brother Ron for his strong arms around our
mother's shoulders, and for proving that humor can be
passed along in the genes. To my mother for the beauty
and courage of her love. And to my father,
for showing us the way home.

# PROLOGUE

When I was about ten years old, my father and I drove out to the ranch my family owned throughout my childhood. It was a bright Saturday morning and we turned off the Pacific Coast Highway onto the familiar mountainous road that would take us to the open land and undeveloped acres of Agoura. On the way out we talked about his horse, Nancy D, and the foal she was about to have. It wasn't a planned pregnancy; an Appaloosa stallion who had been given to my father had broken through two fences to reach Nancy D and had succeeded admirably.

As soon as we drove into the barnyard of our ranch and saw Ray, who took care of the property for us, we knew something was horribly wrong. Tears streaked his face, his eyes were puffy from crying, and he stood in front of my father with his head down, unable to meet his eyes. Nancy D had died during the night from a virus that no one could have known she had. There were no symptoms, no clues; it suddenly and quickly killed her and the colt inside her.

I immediately burst into tears. Nancy D was the first horse I ever sat on. When I was small, my father used to hold me on the saddle in front of him. When I got bigger, he would lift me onto her back and lead me around the ring. She was patient and steady, seeming to know that the small person on her back was young and inexperienced. When I looked up at my father that morning, against the deep blue of the sky, he wasn't crying. He was looking up into all that blue and the expression on his face was sweet and soft . . . and a million miles away.

"Why aren't you crying?" I asked him through my own tears.

He put his hand on my shoulder and met my eyes. "Because," he said, "I'm thinking about all the wonderful times I had with her. We had some great years together."

It was one of my first lessons about death—about looking past it, if only for a few moments, at all the life that went before, all the loveliness and the rich memories. Those are what sustain us, is the lesson my father was trying to impart.

On the day he was dying, I whispered to my father, "You'll see Nancy D again. The two of you will go on long rides just like you used to." I whispered it with the trust he always wanted me to have—that in the stillness of his soul he would hear me.

In the days and weeks since he died, I've often found myself lingering on the image of us standing at the ranch on that bright Saturday morning, my father's eyes tilted up to the sky. His first response to death was to remember the beauty of the life that had passed. The memory comes when I find myself wondering, Where are you?

The larger question aside, I knew one place I would find my father was in the manuscript I had begun in April 1995 and had set aside, after a couple of hundred pages, in February 1997. I'd started writing it as a way to deal with the grief that slammed into me that spring—six months after my father announced to the world that he had been diagnosed with Alzheimer's. I don't know why so many months went by before I crumbled beneath a fate none of us could control. Grief has its own timetable. Maybe there is a mercy to it—a period of shock, numbness. We drift on with the knowledge that life has shifted dramatically but we are unable to fully grab hold of what that means.

In any event, April is when it happened. I began writing a kind of journal—in sleepless nights, in the quiet hush of dawn, sometimes in the back of taxis or at outdoor cafés along Columbus Avenue. I was living in New York and the trees in Central Park were sprouting new leaves. Blossoms were appearing everywhere. The air was warm and billowy. So much new life was around me. Even my relationship with my mother was new. . . .

After many years of a chilly, dispiriting war—one that wounded my father terribly—we had come together lovingly, peacefully, and sadly, joined then in the hard journey of losing my father. It was a journey my mother would call "the Long Goodbye." When I finally realized I was writing a book, there seemed no more appropriate title.

For almost two years, I navigated the pathways of a grief that was new and unfamiliar. I ricocheted between memories, and fear, and a sorrow so vast I didn't know how it would ever be contained. I made a life for myself in New York, I got to know my mother, finally, as I never had before; I traveled back to California as often as I could to spend time with my father. And I wrote—feverishly and often, trying to make sense of the loss that was tugging at my family, that was claiming us and defining us. In how many ways would we lose my father? Who would he be after Alzheimer's cruel surgery? Who would we be after years of watching him be whittled away?

During this time, my sister, Maureen, and I also reached past years of competitiveness and jealousy—mostly over our father—and learned how to be sisters. Our long-distance calls became frequent and affectionate.

She had undergone surgery for melanoma and was on a yearlong treatment of Interferon. It ravaged her, made her ill and weak—too weak to travel from Sacramento, her home, to Los Angeles to see our father. I think she suffered more from that than from the cancer treatment.

In February 1997 I put the manuscript aside. The tumult of my grief was starting to abate; I looked ahead and saw months, maybe years of waiting for an ending that was inevitable. Alzheimer's disease locks all the doors and exits. There is no reprieve, no escape. Time becomes the enemy, and it seemed to stretch out in front of us like miles of fallow land. If I kept adding to the book I had committed myself to, I reasoned, I would end up with a tome of a thousand pages. And much of it would be about the long stretches of waiting—waiting for things to get worse, or end—with we, the loved ones, having nothing but helplessness at our fingertips. In the lexicon of the disease, it's called "plateauing." People with Alzheimer's skate along some strangely level course, not markedly different from one day to the next. It can last for many months. But it's the thinnest of ice they are skating on. The change will come. The fall. The next phase. They will get worse, if death doesn't claim them first.

I moved back to Los Angeles in 1997. Closer to my parents, closer to my father's leaving. Over the next seven years, I wrote for magazines and newspapers and occasionally wrote about what we were going through as a family. Postcards—that's how I think of them. I was increasingly aware of how much the world cared and wanted to know how my father was doing, how we were doing. Alzheimer's came out of the shadows during those years. People talked about it openly, without shame or embarrassment. So I wrote postcards when a particular holiday struck me and evoked memories—something many families are haunted by if Alzheimer's has invaded them. Or when some hairpin turn in our long goodbye begged to be recorded.

During those years, the world of our family changed in some dramatic ways. Maureen was felled again by melanoma, but this time, it was everywhere—racing through her body and conquering everything in its path. She was a valiant opponent, refusing to give up. She was in the John Wayne Cancer Ward at St. John's Hospital in Santa Monica when our father fell and broke his hip in February 2001 and was rushed to the same hospital. Ron flew in from Seattle. We visited Maureen on one floor and our father on the other. Maureen was too ill to go down three flights and see the father she adored. My father probably wouldn't have recognized her even if she had been able to.

My mother would now have to sleep in their bed alone. Her love, her partner for decades, would now have to sleep in a hospital bed; what was once his office would now be his bedroom. Nurses would have to tend to him, and we were told to expect his death in the next few months. None of us expected him to live for another four years—bedridden, with Alzheimer's as his captor.

Maureen died on August 9, 2001—at home in Sacramento with her husband and daughter around her. Our family was growing smaller in so many ways.

The following month the entire world changed. September 11 destroyed more than two towers, more even than the thousands of lives that were lost on that terrible day. It destroyed faith and hope for the future; it killed something vital in all of us. It ripped at the fabric of life as we knew it and left us with a sense of dread that nothing could ever take away.

My mother and I stood at my father's bedside and told him what had happened even though he couldn't consciously absorb it. "Something awful happened to us," I whispered to him. "We're never going to be the same." I missed him more after September 11 than I had in all the years prior to that day, and I had never considered that I could miss him more. But I did. I missed him as a daughter. I knew he would be able to say something to at least let me look beyond—imagine beyond—tears and crippling sorrow to a time when the pain wouldn't be as bad. And I missed him as an American. Our country had been so cruelly wounded. We desperately needed solace and comfort, a guiding hand and a strong, comforting voice . . . and there was no one who could give that to us. My father's voice was silent. The man occupying the Oval Office had no idea how to soothe a grieving nation.

There was a service at the Bel Air Presbyterian Church, and my mother and I went. We sat in the same pew my parents always used to sit in; I sat on the aisle as my father always did. He was claustrophobic; he insisted on aisle seats. I share that affliction with him and was glad to take his seat. When the choir sang "America the Beautiful," tears broke in me. I wept for this country that my father had loved so deeply, the country I had shaken my fist at in the sixties and resented in the eighties for taking him away from me—for making him its father, and for being the more important child. I wept for the man lying in a hospital bed a few miles away, unable to help heal the nation he loved so profoundly. I wept for every person who was suddenly and brutally faced with the loss of someone they loved, cared for, thought they'd see tomorrow. I wished I could tap into what my father would say—I knew it would soothe somehow the wide, raw wounds that were everywhere—but I couldn't. His wisdom, his ability to comfort in times of crisis, had been pirated away by a disease that doesn't care what you can offer the world; it's simply come for you because you were in its path.

TEN DAYS AFTER my father died, I took a box of pages from my bookcase, pages I began in April 1995 and had titled "The Long Goodbye." The morning was foggy; it reminded me of my father's last day—the soft white beginning of it. Slowly, over hours, I read and went back in time. I returned to the daughter who was just starting to grapple with the huge loss of her father—the hole in the world that would never be filled when he left. I didn't know then to what degree Alzheimer's would be a slow prelude to dying, a blurring of everything that was uniquely, essentially my father. In 1995 not too many of us knew what to expect from the disease. We knew it was a wasteland, but what did that mean? We imagined stumbling upon oases, spots of lush green in all those acres of dying. In reading through these pages, I have found moments when both Maureen and I held to that illusion.

The truth of the journey through Alzheimer's is that it doesn't happen like that. Alzheimer's is a scorched earth disease. Nothing you think will remain does. But as soon as I tell you that, I must also tell you that if you are with someone who has Alzheimer's and you pay close attention—if you open wide your heart and your mind—you will see that the disease can never cross the boundaries of the soul. For years I had gentle and true conversations with my father—between his soul and mine, sometimes in total silence. There will be people who say that didn't happen, that it can't happen, it's just a wishful fantasy. Don't believe them.

When I began this book in 1995 I had the naive idea that it was not a book about Alzheimer's—only a book about grief. I was wrong. Alzheimer's is a haunting presence in these pages. The relentless pirate. The thief that steals a human being like nothing else can. The only victory over it is in the realm of the soul. My father proved it in his last moments before dying.

This is still, though, ultimately a story about grieving—about learning how to take those first messy, stumbling steps, about the struggle to keep walking even though the path is shadowy and strewn with unexpected obstacles.

There is some messiness in these pages—I was conflicted about my mother's decision to sell the ranch. I wanted to hold on to everything that belonged to my father, mostly because I couldn't hold on to him. He was leaving. Nothing could return him to us. If I could only hold on to the land he'd loved so much . . .

I was also conflicted about the role of the Reagan Library in our lives. I saw it in much the same way as I used to see America—an institution that owned my parents in ways I couldn't. There was a part of me, all these years later when I read through the manuscript, that wanted to tear up those pages. But I didn't. It's how I felt then, in the tumult of early grief. The story remains as it was in the first telling.

My father is now buried at the library; my mother will be laid to rest there as well. On the final day of a long week of mourning, we stood with miles of sky above us, rolling acres of land below, and I finally understood why my parents fell in love with that mountaintop and why they wanted their legacy to be housed there.

We discover ourselves, assemble our priorities, through beginnings and endings, joys and sorrows. Time carries us like a river and we change along the way. In learning to grieve, we grow into the people we were always meant to be. We look behind to who we were in order to understand who we have become.

We left my father's casket at the library on a blue and gold sunset evening, exactly as he asked us to. But we will never leave him, and he will never be far away from us. The country, the world, will remember a man who loved America, who believed in this land and the hopes it offered. They will remember his respect for the office of the presidency and the dignity with which he treated it.

As his daughter, I will remember his strong arms lifting me onto the back of a horse and how he taught me that one of the most important things was to get back on whenever I fell off so fear wouldn't set in. I will remember him in the ocean, teaching me how to ride waves into shore, or swim straight toward them so I could slide down their backs and make it out to calmer waters. I will remember how he knew the skies—how he could point out Pegasus, the Big Dipper, Orion . . . and how he always knew where the North Star was. It guides sailors home, he told me once when I was a child and we were visiting my grandparents in Chicago. If you're ever lost, look up and find the North Star.

He taught me to look up—on that clear Chicago night when I was so young that my father could never figure out how I remembered it at all. On a California morning with sun like butterscotch spilling across our shoulders and the horse he loved so much gone, taken in the middle of the night. He taught me to look up.

I'm trying to be a good student. I wake in the quietest hours of night, usually around three a.m. I don't know why, I just do. And like the sailors he told me about, I am drifting, without direction or bearings. I want to know where my father is. So I go to the window and I find the North Star in the sky. That's what he told me to do if I was ever lost and couldn't find my way home.

My father always believed in going home.

# THE LONG GOODBYE

## APRIL 1995

When I got married in 1984, my father gave a toast at my wedding. I don't remember his exact words, but they had to do with his recollection of how tiny my hand once was, as a child holding on to his, and how so many years later, he was giving my hand in marriage. An older hand, a woman's hand.

These days, I find myself looking at my father's hands. They seem to have grown smaller, a bit more frail. It's as if they no longer need to grasp life, stretch themselves around it; rather, they are learning to let it go. It's a soft release, not like the Dylan Thomas poem I once embraced: "Do not go gentle into that good night, / Old age should burn and rave at close of day."

I still like that poem; I like its fury and its fierce passion. But I think my father's way is sweeter.

I watch his eyes these days, too. They shimmer across some unfathomable distance, content to watch from wherever his mind has alighted. If I turn into his eyes, it's like turning into a calm breeze. The serenity is contagious.

The tendency when you're around someone with Alzheimer's is to try to reel them back in, include them in the conversation, pique their interest in whatever you happen to be discussing. But I stopped doing that because it seemed to me that I was intruding. Wherever he was, he was content. Wherever he was, he shouldn't be disturbed.

At the ranch we owned when I was younger, my father taught me that when a horse was growing older, when riding it would be unkind and possibly harmful, the horse should be allowed a more peaceful life, roaming in the acres of pasture that our ranch provided. I remember several of our horses living out the remainder of their days in wide, green fields, grazing. That's how I think of my father now; it's what I see in his eyes. Things are calmer where he is—most of the time, anyway. And he grazes—on the moments and hours that are left to him. On the sight of afternoon sun gilding the lawn or clouds skimming across the sky. On his family, who have finally learned how to laugh together, and how to love. He grazes on the taste of life as it slips away—the rich, fertile moments that must be released into the wind, because that's what you do if you're like my father, his hand reaching for God's, leaving ours behind, saying goodbye in small ways, getting us used to his absence.

I haven't read any of the books on Alzheimer's. I probably should, but I don't want my thoughts to be cluttered with other people's impressions, or with medical predictions and evaluations. I want to keep watching my father's hands. I want to remember how they've changed, how uncallused and tender they've become. And I want to chart his distance from his eyes. They're a map, but you have to look closely. Sometimes, I think I actually see him leaving, retreating, navigating his way out of this world and into the next. Other times, I see him right there, as if he's preserving each moment under glass.

When daylight saving time dictated that we should

move our clocks ahead an hour, I thought of my father. My mother said that the first clock she changed was his watch. He looks at his watch often now—I'm not sure why. Is it that time seems to be moving faster, and he wants to chase after it by marking its passage? Or does each time of day now have a special significance? Either way, losing an hour of time must have had more of an impact on him than it did on most of us. Life is measured in time—in years, months, hours. And one hour just vanished. It wasn't wasted; it wasn't squandered by daydreaming or staring out the window. It was snatched away, erased—because someone decided it should be. I try to see things sometimes as he must. He lives more in the moment now. It's one thing I have learned about Alzheimer's—the past and the future are risky subjects. It occurs to me that it must seem unfair to him that a precious hour—a measurement of life—could so easily be discarded, erased from the map of time. Yet it also occurs to me that, in one way, he is living as we all should—in the present moment.

I hold on to this as a tiny gift in the midst of a sad time. I suppose it's what happens when one sees a horizon darkened by disease or loss—there are always thin rays of light. You have to be on the alert for them, and hold on tightly to them.

## MAY 1995, LOS ANGELES

On Sunday morning, I went to church with my parents. It's something my father looks forward to all week, and I wanted to share the experience; I wanted to watch him, absorb some of his reverence.

He remembers every word of the Lord's Prayer. He was looking straight ahead, to the pulpit and the tall wooden cross behind it, reciting the prayer along with everyone else, never missing a syllable. The same thing happened with the doxology: "Praise God from whom all blessings flow . . ." He sang it perfectly.

I thought about the mysteries of this thing we call memory. Even being encroached upon by something as relentless as Alzheimer's, the memory has pockets that resist the progression of time and the steady march of disease. It's fitting that, in my father's case, those pockets contain hymns and prayers. They are his treasures; they always have been—the shiny stones he turns over in his hand, keeping them polished and smooth. I closed my eyes for a moment as I sat between my parents and prayed that he will always be able to recite the Lord's Prayer, always recall a hymn. I asked God to keep his treasures safe.

MY MOTHER AND I talk about death now as if we are resigning ourselves to its presence, growing more comfortable with having it around, lurking nearby. At the moment, it's a shadow on the wall, but one that's lengthening, one that won't go home at dawn. I'm reminded of Don Juan's counsel in Carlos Castaneda's books. He said that death is our constant companion, that it travels on our left shoulder, and that our task must be to make it our "ally."

I feel, in my conversations with my mother, that we are both making friends with this shadowy presence, this unwelcome guest. Because the enemy—the true messenger of terror—would be the full progression of Alzheimer's. I never want to see the day when my father stands up in church and is unable to remember the Lord's Prayer. I would rather watch him turn toward his left shoulder and say, "All right, I'm ready now."

Frequently these days, my mother and I remind each other that the grieving process has already begun. It's a mountainous journey, and we need to be reassured that we've already covered some miles. It's as if we are passing a canteen of water back and forth—it doesn't shorten the distance, but it helps.

When I say "I love you" to my father now, I'm deliberate and focused about it. I say it straight into his eyes, straight into the deepest currents of his soul. I want the words to be like those of the Lord's Prayer—ones he won't forget, ones that will resist the onslaught of disease.

We all have a passage out of this world and into the

next. This is my father's, as sad as it is for those of us around him who don't want anything to be wrong with him. But ultimately, it will be his passage home. That's what he always told me: God will come to each of us when he's ready, and he will take us home.

My father made heaven sound so lovely—a peaceful, green kingdom in which all living creatures get along. A celestial Noah's Ark. When one of my fish died, he and I scooped it out of the aquarium and gave it a funeral. My father tied sticks together to form a cross, which he placed on the tiny grave; he gave my fish a brief eulogy and described to me the clear blue waters it would be swimming in up in heaven. I could see the water—blue as the sky, endless, and teeming with other fish, none of whom would eat one another. I became so enchanted with this vision that I felt sorry for my other fish, condemned to the small, unnatural environment of the aquarium, with its colored rocks and gray plastic castle.

"Maybe we should kill the others," I said to my father, eager to give them the same freedom, the same beauty as my newly departed fish.

He told me, in God's time, the others would go too.

I go back to childhood to retrieve the stories that once made me feel better, hoping that they still have the same effect. I became less certain as I got older. When did I stop imagining a green-and-blue paradise on the other side? When did fear throw it in shadow? I need to return to the stories in order to let my father go.

## JUNE 1995

My mother and I each have a friend who is ill. We watch helplessly as both struggle against failing bodies. Her friend's body is ravaged by cancer; my friend, HIV-positive for over ten years, is now battling a steady onslaught of illnesses, infections, and diseases. The latest demon is lymphoma. He might recover, if the chemo doesn't destroy him. Her friend will not.

For weeks, she and I have been exchanging information, sharing our experiences, our thoughts, our fears. Looming behind these conversations is always the eventuality of my father's death. It has occurred to me more than once that when we're discussing her friend or mine we are, by extension, also talking about my father. We are wading into a murky lake that's going to get deeper before we reach the other side. We're stocking up for the journey, preparing ourselves.

MY MOTHER FLEW in to New York for a few days this week. She scheduled as much as she could into that brief time, as people usually do who don't live here. New York becomes a whirlwind experience for visitors; for the rest of us, it moves at a more even pace. One of the reasons she came now is her friend's failing health; there might not be another chance to see him.

On Sunday, we had brunch together before going over to this man's apartment, where he has been living out his last days. In the dining room of the Carlyle Hotel, I told my mother about a recent dream I had. In it, my father was bleeding from his hand; he had it raised in the air, and blood was streaming down his arm. I was trying to help him, but he kept assuring me that everything was fine, there was no need to worry. Then he vanished, and I couldn't find him. The Secret Service agents told me he had been taken to a hospital, but they didn't know which one. I was desperate to find him. In the midst of this, I saw a tour being conducted through my childhood home—a long line of tourists and visitors coming to view our lives. The dream felt biblical—wounds to the hand—and disjointed, scattered. It was one of those dreams that stay with me for days.

When we came into her friend's apartment, it felt like the home of someone who knew he was going to die. Old, wilted flowers were in a vase in the living room, and a tired-looking houseplant had drooped from lack of water. He was waiting for us in the den, propped up in an armchair with pillows behind him, water and medicines within easy reach. He looked like my friend—gaunt, with those wide, questioning eyes that try to reach beyond the limits of vision and then just as quickly turn inward. As I sat with my mother and one of her oldest friends, I thought that it ultimately doesn't matter which disease gnaws away at the body—it looks the same. The flesh surrenders, grows exhausted, and the eyes ask why.

"What am I going to do without you?" my mother asked at one point.

"Oh, you'll manage," he answered, but there was another conversation going on beneath the words. They were saying goodbye to each other.

I knew my mother was fighting back tears. I knew because three days earlier I had sat in my friend's hospital room doing the same thing. On the fourteenth floor of Roosevelt Hospital, he looked out the window, paused, and said in a soft voice, "Sometimes I wonder why I fight so hard to live. This world is so hard." I had no answer, just the pressure of tears behind my eyes.

Days later, I sat beside my mother in her friend's apartment. The living room was cluttered with valuable artwork—the collections of a lifetime. He looked into the distance and said, "I just don't understand this. I don't know what's happening to me." She also had no answer, although I think, in her silence, there was an exchange. They had known each other for thirty years; words weren't always required.

When his housekeeper came in with more water for him, he asked if we wanted anything; we both declined. Then he looked at me and said, "Are you sure I can't get you anything? Tea? Water? A Rembrandt?" Humor can find a way in, even through the bleakest times. My friend has done this too, astonishing me at times with his willingness to laugh.

I didn't know what to say to my mother when we left her friend's apartment building. I put my arm around her shoulders as we walked out into bright sunlight. We both knew this had been a final goodbye. Eventually, we talked about it, but haltingly. Words seem frail when the emotions are so huge, so cumbersome, that they defy order, lumber over any attempt to string them into sentences.

Yet writing has been the one constant in my life; it's anchored me, flooded me, made me want to survive. So I race to find a scrap of paper—anything to write on—afraid that I'll forget something, panicked that a singular, stunning moment might go unrecorded.

MY CONVERSATIONS WITH my mother move from high blue spheres of spirit to the hard, unforgiving surface of earth. We talk about death as a continuum, a relocating of the soul, a journey to a better place. We talk about the cord binding hearts that have loved; we assure each other that it remains intact in the passage between worlds. We are talking about my father, her husband of forty-three years. Eventually, the earth comes up to meet us, slams into us. We can't seem to stay above it.

My mother speaks of the loneliness of her life now. He's here, but in so many ways, he's not. She feels the loneliness in small ways—he used to put lotion on her back; now he doesn't. And in the huge, overwhelming ways—a future that will be spent missing him.

SMALL, MUNDANE THINGS seem fraught with meaning. I feel as if I'm living in a constant state of metaphor. When we had brunch together, my mother and I both ordered asparagus. I told her that years ago, in California, when I had a large vegetable garden, I discovered that asparagus sends up stalks only every other year. In the off years, it waits beneath the soil, gathering strength. As I told her this, I thought of our family, our memories—the deepest ones that wait and draw strength from the soil. In years of heavy rain, I got asparagus that was thick as giants' toes. The stalks poked out of the earth, straight and defiant, gloriously green. For my family, this is a year of heavy tears, and our memories burst from the soil in stunning color. They fill our conversations. My mother recalls how my father used to count out vitamins for her when they were going on a trip, making sure she had enough for each day, so that she wouldn't get a cold. I remember riding on my father's back across the swimming pool, like a frog riding on the back of a dolphin. I can still feel the chlorine sting in my eyes, still see the afternoon sun moving across the sky, throwing one corner of the pool into shadow—I called it the Amazon. During the years when I had my vegetable garden, I plucked dinner from the soil; now we pluck memories from the years we have shared. We need their sustenance.

For more than forty years, my mother has rolled into my father in the gray stillness of dawn, waking to the scent of his skin, the heat of his body beside her. Her lover, her husband, for all these decades—my lifetime. It's almost unfathomable to me, the loss she must be wrestling with. Yet it is fathomable because I've lived long enough to know loss, to feel the gulf it leaves inside. And I have no words for it.

I can't find the words to lift my mother back up to those clear, blue heights.

I know, in part, I'm experiencing the strange, almost-mystical shift that often happens in parent-child relation-ships. I'm trying to cradle my mother's sorrow, be mother to the small, tentative voice that reveals her fears.

It's particularly poignant because I am part of a gen-eration that rebelled against the idea of being anyone's child, and I was one of its voices. Many of us are now seeing the tables turn, the roles reverse. Older, we step out of the shadows and sing lullabies to our parents, melodies recalled from the very childhoods we railed against. We are being invited, by circumstance and by the relentless passage of time, to be more tender, more loving, than we've been in the past.

My mother said that when her mother died, she real-ized she was "nobody's little girl anymore." The protective arms that had made the world a safer place were gone. She was standing exposed. "One step closer to the abyss" is how another friend phrased it. I listen carefully now to friends who have lost one or both of their parents. There are common threads running through their experiences. It was more wrenching, more of a jolt, for them to get to what my mother saw immediately. They first had to retrieve their childhoods, embrace the idea that they had always been their parents' child; only then came the sad realization that they were nobody's child anymore.

So we light lanterns and leave them on the road behind us for those coming after. We help each other learn to grieve, to love, to reach out to parents we once pushed away. For a generation that took so long to grow up, it's some of the best work we can do.

## LATE JUNE 1995

My mother is part of a generation of women who became accustomed to veils. The gentle lifting of a white wedding veil symbolized a transformative moment in a girl's life. There were the hats worn by screen legends and fashionable women—with fishnet-woven veils pulled delicately down over the eyes. In my generation, we have made it our mission to discard veils. We get married on mountaintops in thrift-store satin slips, with bare feet and bare faces. We wear Greta Garbo hats with demure veils only to costume parties. Our mothers have adapted to the times as well as they can, but they hold on to the more invisible veils—those that conceal the chaos and pain of life, the clutter of emotions that come along with just being alive. They compose themselves, put on brave faces, while we, having been weaned on primal therapy, look for a support group where we can scream it out. They probably scream it out, too, at some point . . . but they pull the curtains first. So it's stunning when the blinds are left open, when the veils are dropped.

My mother's friend died this morning. I went with her to his apartment with the expectation that we would get there in time—that she would be able to say goodbye, tell him she loved him, watch his eyelids flutter one last time, and perhaps close them when they went still. We were ten minutes too late.

Two other friends were there—women who, along with my mother, were then faced with the rambling, unwieldy task of attending to the business of death. I was witness to the veils dropping. There was nothing to hide, nothing to hide behind, and no reason to want to. Death is not delicate. His body lay in bed with the air conditioner humming and the sweltering New York day pressing down on the city outside the window. My mother held his hand—still warm—kissed his forehead, and told him she loved him. I'm sure she left tears there. The phone kept ringing; things had to be attended to. The lawyer had to be called, along with the doctor, the undertaker, the rabbi.

Everywhere I turned in his apartment there were memories—photographs, treasures, a shopping bag from Williams-Sonoma. It seemed such a small thing, yet it held my attention—one of those daily errands, like dry cleaning or cat food. You put it down in the hallway or by the bookcase, where it doesn't belong, with the intention of coming back for it. Except life has other plans. It plans to end—at least life as we think of it, life that includes dry cleaning, and cat food, and bags of culinary tools from Williams-Sonoma.

My mother had seen someone dead before; I had not. But there was something peaceful about it. I was sure I felt his soul floating around in the air-conditioned bedroom where he'd spent so many long days and nights in pain. I imagined him enjoying his weightlessness. He had drifted off to fairer weather; the storm of his passing was left to this trinity of women—his friends—who had to balance missing him with taking care of the business at hand.

On this somber, chaotic morning, I felt more acquainted with death; it moved closer to birth. I felt the cycle turning back into itself, forming a perfect sphere. We arrive in this world veiled—the caul over a baby's head, shed from the mother's womb—and we leave veiled. I'm sure someone pulled the sheet over her friend's face, although I didn't go back in to look. In death, as in birth, there are screams and tears, and awe at the fierce majesty of it all. If we're lucky, we step up to those raw, blinding moments with a gentle, immense courage. We drop veils; we cry; we laugh at the sweet memories and shake our heads in disbelief that they pass so quickly. And we hold on tightly to those around us. Because you never know.

My mother would have had to extend her visit for three days to go to the service. Everyone understood that she didn't want to be away from my father for an extra few days. I had another thought which I didn't ask her about—she will tell me if she wants. It had to do with missing the moment of her friend's death by those ten minutes. Time away from my father means moments missed, and life can change at lightning speed. I believe she got to her friend's apartment when she was supposed to, and the moment of my father's passing will also happen as it is supposed to.

I have said this to my mother, but I feel again the inadequacy of words. They seem, at moments, like the Popsicle-stick forts I used to build as a child—they're good until a wind blows in.

# July 1995

My mother has called it a long goodbye—the way Alzheimer's slowly steals a person away. It's been one of her only public comments; upon agreement, we have chosen the cloak of respectful silence when it comes to the subject of my father's condition. It's a heartbreaking phrase, and she's told me she won't say it again because it ushers in tears.

I just finished a book tour for *Angels Don't Die* and didn't take enough time for tears. My time was spent sleeping on planes, in strange hotel rooms, riffling through a suitcase I never had a chance to unpack, and racing from one interview to the next. For the most part the interviews themselves were kind, supportive; I wondered how I had survived the combat of past book tours when I had, through my own choices as a writer, put myself in the line of fire. It seems predictable, though, that even in the best book tours, there is always one interview that leaves you shaking your head in bewilderment at the interviewer's crassness.

It happened in one of the smaller cities, which I won't name. It was an afternoon talk show. The woman who was hosting the show—an Oprah wannabe who will never be—asked me how my father was.

My answer to that question never varied from one interview to the next. "He's doing well," I said. "My family has asked for a zone of privacy around specific details of his condition. But he's doing well."

Usually, that was enough; no one else had pressed further. "Well, does he remember you? Can you have a conversation with him?" she asked, apparently feeling perfectly justified in asking the private questions I'd already said I wasn't going to answer.

"As I said, we have asked for a zone of privacy, which I think we're entitled to."

"When exactly did you discover that he had Alzheimer's? Did you start to notice him forgetting things or getting mixed up?"

"You're asking questions which I've already made clear I'm not going to answer," I told her, a little more firmly. I could feel the discomfort of the live audience; she gave it another try.

"What is a conversation with him like these days? What can you talk about?"

"This is the fourth time I've given the same response, and it's going to be the last. We have asked for a zone of privacy. No matter how many different ways you phrase the same question, I'm not going to answer you."

The audience applauded, and she—finally—moved on to another line of questioning.

At the end of the show, as I was heading anxiously for the exit, she said, "I hope you understand; I was just doing my job as a journalist."

I don't think I answered her.

The other difficulty of this book tour was a sweet one in a way, even though it was sad. Again and again, in talking about my father and the book I had written about him, I had to recall the luster of memories, the deep rivers of his faith, the manna of his storytelling. The phrase "long goodbye" whispered through my mind constantly, like a stream of wind through a house when a door has been left open. The tears I needed to cry and couldn't find time for formed a pool inside me—a patient, deep pond that waited for me to get to it. Once I got back to New York, all I wanted to do was sleep and cry.

In a way, this book tour brought me face-to-face with the life I've lived until recently, the choices I made in the past, my long years of battle with my parents. I phoned my mother from greenrooms before interviews, from hotel rooms, airports; she is part of my life now, but I could see all those years of exile like a wasteland stretching behind me.

Fame is a strange phenomenon; it always surprises you even if you've grown up around it. You think you have it figured out; you have your priorities in order, your choices thought out and clear. Most of us have made mistakes, but I think the first moment that the spotlight turns on you is the most crucial; no mistakes are weightier than the ones made then. It's a golden moment, and it will never come again. There will be other moments—I don't believe we only have one chance to get it right—but it will never be that pure again, that unencumbered.

I was twenty-eight when my father was elected president, and my family was caught up in a media whirlwind, unfamiliar in its intensity even though we were not strangers to the spotlight. Obviously, it all happened because of my father, but the rest of us were in that spotlight as well. My first mistake was thinking I could handle it. If I had been more hesitant, less sure, I'd have asked more questions, considered more options. As it turned out, I proceeded with evangelical fervor; passionate about my political beliefs, I spoke at huge antinuclear rallies, sat for interviews, presented myself as one of the most conspicuous opponents of my father's policies. If I had been more diplomatic, less strident, I actually might have become a bridge between my father's politics and the liberal viewpoint. Instead, I was just an angry daughter, even in the eyes of those who shared my political beliefs.

I followed those first angry gestures with more personal ones, feeling it was my duty to let the world in on my family's wounds. My anger invited anger from others; to say I got hate mail is an understatement.

Because much of this was played out on book tours, I couldn't exactly escape my past. Everyone grows, changes, learns, but it's harder to go through that process publicly. People, for the most part, have been supportive, forgiving, but their memories are long—I see it in their eyes. That's what's difficult about doing your growing in public: you're always running into someone else's memories of you.

In my imagination, I talk to my father about this; I tell him how I wish I had handled things differently. Maybe our opposing views could have been a revelation to each of us instead of a battle. And in my imagination, his eyes shine, and he smiles and nods. He says something like "I'm glad we can talk about it now." But that conversation can take place only in my imagination; the part of him that could attend it in real life is far away.

• • •

WITH A DISEASE like Alzheimer's, the wilderness belongs also to friends, loved ones, those who bear witness and will be left behind to grieve. You watch a person retreat to a strange land, knowing you can't follow. But the absence leaves you wandering in a wilderness all your own. You catch echoes bouncing off mountainsides, and you stop to listen. They're only echoes—the voice they came from is growing quiet—so you listen more carefully.

"I remember . . ." is how many of my mother's sentences begin these days.

You breathe life into your own memories because right there, in front of you, sitting in the chair he always goes to, or walking down the hall, or gazing out the window, is a reminder of the hollowness that's left when memories are erased. So you welcome it when images come back, or bits of conversation. You seize them, dust them off, and pray they'll stay as bright.

Often now I think of the stories I would like to hear again in my father's voice, in the blue twinkle of his eyes that delighted in feeding a child's imagination. But I have to nourish myself on echoes. I want him to tell me again how to distinguish a hawk from a buzzard. There are subtle differences in their flight paths, their wings. One circles longer before diving down for its prey. I used to get them mixed up frequently, and he would patiently explain it to me again or point out the differences if we were at the ranch and he spotted either of the birds overhead. I still get them mixed up, but I can't ask him; he no longer remembers. I want us to mount horses and ride off over the slope of green hills, but he will never again get on a horse.

Once, when we were on our way to the ranch, driving

along Mulholland, he stopped the car to tell a man up on
the hillside that the blue lupine he was picking was a protected plant. My father explained it politely, and the man
climbed down from the hill, clutching his one illegal
flower. My father believed in leaving flowers and wildlife
where they belonged, whenever possible. I could identify a
rattlesnake by the age of five; I knew to avoid them, to
make a wide circle around them. And I knew to never kill
one unless it was absolutely necessary.

Never before have I longed this deeply for childhood—just a taste of it, a wafer on my tongue, a sweet
communion with a past that's lost to me now. Adults look
backward with a sad wisdom; we remember how, as children, we were blissfully unaware of life's determined
march, the countdown of years. It seemed impossible that
time would etch itself into our flesh. Looking back, we
wish we had held on tighter to certain moments, stared a
little longer into someone's face or into a spectacular
sunset, listened more carefully to a voice that would one
day be stilled. We wish we had moved more slowly, lingered longer, turned down different roads. We preserve
things in memory and hope they won't crumble or fade,
because they are testaments to the life we've lived.

When we say goodbye to a loved one, the goodbye
isn't only to the person who is leaving; it's to the stories,
the information gathered over the course of a lifetime. My
father is taking small but certain steps away from who he
once was. I wonder what else I might have learned from
him—about the land, about horses, the flight paths of
birds, plants that thrive only in certain areas. He could
find a plant in the oak grove at the ranch that, when wet,
lathered like soap.

He believed in preparing his children for life's mishaps, its shocks and hairpin turns that can be devastating if you are not prepared. He would give us scenarios, ask us what we would do, and then gently correct us so that, if disaster struck, knowledge would be our ally.

He asked me once, "What would you do if there was a fire in your bedroom, blocking the doorway?"

Having watched way too many movies, I said, "I'd run through it."

"You'd be dead," my father answered calmly. "The heat would sear your lungs once you got within two feet of the flames."

"I'd break the window and go out into the yard."

"Okay," he said, nodding. "How would you break the window?"

"A chair."

I could always tell when the important part of the lesson was coming up. My father would lean in, speak slowly and carefully, anxious for the information to take root. "You take out one of your drawers," he told me, "and push it through the window. That way, you get a clean break, and you won't cut yourself climbing out."

He prepared me for fires, air-raid warnings, earthquakes. But he didn't prepare me for losing him. He gave me no tools to deal with the cold wash of regret—the times I turned away from him, brushed aside his outstretched hand, chose words that were sharp as spears. Those memories are mine to harbor; if there is a remedy for them, I haven't found it.

The story of losing a parent often includes discovery. You open a drawer, a book, a box of letters, and learn something about that parent you didn't know before.

Thoughts are scrawled in the margins of a book he or she loved, or you stumble across a letter your eyes weren't meant to see. Sometimes we learn about our parents when they are gone. My mother has been going through drawers—conscious, I think, of the public part of our lives, of the world's prying eyes. She wants to know what others might find. In one of my father's drawers, she found a letter to me—a rough draft—which he never sent. It was written just before my autobiography was published, and he was expressing his hurt at my anger, his wish for our family's reconciliation, his memories of more loving times. At the start of the letter, he said, "With myself going on eighty-one years . . ." And then he crossed out his age and wrote above the line "now eighty-one years . . ."

I imagine him taking out the letter—maybe many times—as days lumbered on, and he felt his life running out. I'll never know how often he took it out, added to it, reread it; nor will I know why he never sent it. His closing line was "Please, Patti, don't take away our memories of a daughter we truly love and whom we miss."

The letter is in my drawer now. The silence around it feels vast—I wish I could talk to him about it, but the memory might as well have fallen off the edge of the earth.

When people leave, they take private, personal mysteries with them—candle flames of happy memories, the broken bones of sad ones. They leave, and it all goes with them. The rest of us are left in darkness with questions we never got around to asking, words we were just about to say but couldn't, because we got there too late.

. . .

THE TASK OF SPEAKING about this long good-bye has fallen to me. These days need to be recorded because for all their weight, there is a grandeur to them. We reach past the pain for succor, our hands as eager as if they were reaching for the Holy Grail. We don't quite touch it, but we know it's there. I am refining the art of holding back tears. I store them with the pride of a wild animal and then retreat to my cave in order to give them their rightful place, to honor their birthright. This long journey is a loosening of the certainties that once seemed stitched together—the fabric of another human being, the person we came to know. You get used to surprises with a disease like this—puzzling phrases and sudden turns. You count on nothing, yet breathe easier at what is familiar. Always, it's a waiting game.

Even without the complication of disease, for those in their eighties the tunnel is narrowing. My father felt it years ago when he wrote that letter to me. I wonder sometimes how it will happen—when I'll get the news. In the middle of the night? At dawn? Whenever it is, however, in my heart I feel my father's passage will be a peaceful one.

Yesterday, I fell asleep on my acupuncturist's table, with needles sticking out of me, strategically placed along meridians that were blocked, or short-circuited, or otherwise confused. I dropped off an edge into deep, black sleep—the kind that brings vivid dreams, almost frightening in their intensity. I saw my father step away from himself; he left his eighty-four-year-old self and emerged as a younger, more vibrant man, with a radiant smile. Robust and enthusiastic, he walked over to my mother with open arms and assured her that everything would be all right.

Eventually, it will be, although things will be different. Out past the grief and the horrible, relentless ache, life will settle into some sort of pattern. For now, there is the waiting. It's like counting the seconds after a lightning flash, waiting for the clap of thunder that you know will come, trying to determine how far away the storm is.

## Late July 1995

When my father taught me how to bodysurf, when he explained to me the majesty of the ocean and the respect I must always have for it, he told me that if a wave was about to break on me, I could dive down and wait out the swell in the calmer waters far below.

These days I find myself diving down to calmer waters deep within my soul. There are those places in the soul that are still, silent, soft as water. I feel very much like I did when I hovered near the ocean's sandy bottom. I knew that, above me, a wave was crashing, but around me the water only swayed a little; there was no churning or somersault currents.

It's that calm I dive down for now—in small moments and sometimes for entire days. I've grown quieter, more withdrawn, even from friends, who I hope understand. I head for the deep reservoirs of strength I know my soul harbors. Because I'll need them. Because I need them now.

My mother is learning to take life one day at a time. It's the choreography that must be learned by anyone who is watching disease encroach upon someone they love. It seems like a formless, unpredictable dance. The chaos comes from the uncertainty. There are good days, bad days, and days that hover in some kind of limbo—days when all you can do is wait. It's a turbulent sea, and you have to stay on the surface, with an eye out for waves. At the other end of the country, I feel tossed about by the same sea.

My mother told me that a few weeks ago, when the moon was full, she went out into the garden late at night and stared up at it. I saw that same moon three thousand miles away, dangling between buildings as I was walking home. In New York, you have to remember to look up; the city levels your gaze, and full moons can go unnoticed. I thought of her in the garden, with the sky wide and unob-structed above her, a sleeping house behind. I pictured her drinking in the elixir of moonlight, learning to be alone. She doesn't come to this easily—the solitariness of watch-ing the moon with nothing but the night air around her. My mother feels most comfortable with companionship. She spends a lot of time on the phone, once joked that she should be buried with a phone in her hand. I could never imagine her needing to take a walk by herself.

My father didn't resist solitude; in fact, he seemed born for it. That strange reserve which made people reach for him. He would respond with a friendly, gregarious openness, but the reserve was still there. People saw it, sensed it, were fascinated by it. My brother and I have the same reserve; inherited, probably, it shows in our eyes, in the time we carve out for ourselves. But I'm not sure ours has the same magic that my father's seemed infused with.

I remember my father sitting at his desk, writing, or staring out the window, stringing words together in his head. There was such a self-contained serenity to it. Often, he would go to the ranch and ride alone along the trails. He said once it was how he cleared his head, made decisions, including the decision to run for president.

It's when we are the most alone that we find our courage. Left alone with our own heartbeat, we resolve to live, take chances, take another step. Our deepest self knows this and insists on being heard. It calls us out into the night, to the silver coin of moon in the late-night sky. It insists that we feel the emptiness of the dark, the whisper of wind. In those moments, we are our most pure, our most naked, and as hard as we might try to avoid them, those moments will find us. My mother is getting to know herself, standing alone and small under the vastness of the sky, the hypnotic glow of the moon. It's how she will learn to survive.

A few weeks ago, when she was in New York, there was a huge thunderstorm on the night she arrived—a chain of them, actually, rolling over Manhattan. They woke me up, and I opened the curtains, amazed at the majesty and drama being played out in the heavens. I assumed my mother's plane had already landed, but I hoped she wasn't in a car somewhere between JFK and the city.

As it turned out, she was in her hotel room, in front of the window, also watching the storm. I thought of what it is we are doing when we stop and watch nature perform for us. We allow ourselves to shrink in its presence; we have no choice, really; its grandeur in moments of unharnessed power is beyond our reach. As we seem to grow smaller, so do our sorrows, our problems, at least for a brief time.

When my mother described how she pulled back the

curtains and sat in the dark, alone, watching rain and flashes of lightning, I knew she would rather have been watching it with my father. Each time she comes to New York, the solitude of her hotel suite strikes her, sounds a note of what the future holds.

"I look around, and I think, This is how it's going to be," she has said.

She must have missed him terribly on that night, when God and nature collaborated to put on such a spectacular show.

Across town, I felt the sting of solitude also—the longing to share the experience with someone I loved. Besides being witnesses to the storm, my mother and I had solitude in common . . . except we have come to this aloneness from opposite directions.

I told her once, recently, "You're so lucky to have known great love in your life. For almost half your life, you have been deeply in love. Unless I fall in love tomorrow and live a very long time, I will never know what you've known."

"I have been lucky," she answered, a bit wistfully. "I hear stories about other marriages, other relationships where there is so much tension, and I know how blessed I've been."

We don't think of our parents' being in love when we're younger. When I was seventeen, I fell in love for the first time. He was much older than I, married, and I didn't tell my parents until it was over, several years later. I didn't think they would understand. Now my mother shows me love letters my father wrote to her. They are yellowed around the edges; the paper feels like it might crumble in my hands. Some were written before I was born; one written just after, when he was on a trip for General Electric, doing what he was contracted to do—represent its products. Now I know how well my parents understood love, how willingly they gave themselves to it, let it encircle them. I compare, perhaps unfairly, my own relationships, and I feel that I have never loved that completely, with that kind of abandon. I always held something back.

Great love, when you're in it or when you witness it, is both simple and terrifyingly complex. Its existence can't be negotiated, nor its intricacies navigated. It requires faith and a brave heart. And it can be both a blessing and a curse. I see in my father's eyes now, at times, a longing to leave this world, to outrun the disease that's chasing him down. But his love for my mother holds him here. And she—a woman whose life has been bonded, twinned, woven inextricably into the life of the man she has loved, is facing a future without him. It must seem to her like a black-night parachute drop into alien territory. You can survive it, part of me wants to tell her. But I know her heart will never be the same.

I wonder if I might end up teaching my mother how to be alone, how to endure the sad interplay of feelings when full-moon nights and the splendor of thunderstorms make her reach out to no one there. I don't know if that can be taught. Maybe all that can be taught is raw survival.

She has a friend who recently lost her husband, and this woman told my mother that the worst time was the period of waiting, the limbo state of watching a disease progress, the first few miles down grief's back roads. Tonight, my mother told me how her own body is mirroring her emotions—a shakiness, a feeling that her head is swimming, off-balance. I hung up the phone and walked into the kitchen, feeling suddenly light-headed. I have had girlfriends with whom I was so connected our menstrual cycles began to coincide. It might be like that, I thought, holding up my hand to see if it was steady, wondering how far this could go. When my mother was last in New York, her stomach was bothering her; almost immediately, I began to get queasy every time I ate. Last night, we talked about life without my father—how frightening it is to her—and I asked her something which had been pulling at me for a while.

"Is there a part of you that wants to go with him?"

"No," she answered quickly—too quickly, I thought. "No, I've never thought that."

"It's okay if you have," I assured her. "It would be perfectly natural. It's a thought; there's nothing wrong with it. I just thought we should talk about it if—"

"No," she said again. "That hasn't even occurred to me."

"Okay. Well, you'll tell me if it does, though—right?"

"Yes," she said.

But I wonder. My parents have never been separated, even when they have been apart. In my childhood, when my father was on short business trips, his nightly phone calls were dependable and lengthy. In the White House years, the closeness of my parents' relationship was often the subject of news stories. It has guided their lives, and, somehow, it will determine the future.

· · ·

FOR THE PAST WEEK, while a cruel heat wave has tortured the city, I've found myself crawling deeper into my internal cave. There is something feral about it, as if I'm hibernating to prepare myself for the next season; something wild, primal, as if I'm gathering food and storing it in my cave so I'll have sustenance when I need it the most.

New York is tolerant of people walking the streets deep in their own thoughts. But I peek out, read those around me. A construction worker I passed this morning said, "How's your father doing?"

"He's well," I answered. "Thanks." It's my standard reply these days.

I had the feeling that this stranger was waiting too—for the inevitable sad ending. Death, when it brushes past us, is a reminder that some things are not negotiable, not subject to our will. Endings are carved deep into stone and earth; pilgrims that we are, we reach them eventually.

I have moments, like the one this morning, when I'm acutely aware of the intimacy of this world. In the interstice between a public and a private life, there is a strange blending of the two, a place where the collective heartbeat of the world matches your own. It isn't only my family that is watching and praying—it's so many others. Sometimes I hear them breathing in my ear, tiptoeing past the door, telling me they're waiting along with us.

## AUGUST 1995, LOS ANGELES

More and more, I feel as if I have two homes. New York is the home I've chosen, but Los Angeles is the home I'm rediscovering. I know each time I go back to California I change a little. It's as if my past and my present are blending together, winding around each other to form new roadways, wider paths.

At my parents' house, I looked at more photographs and scrapbooks, traveling backward in time but looking through the eyes of the woman I've become.

My father was so young. There were pictures of our summer vacations at a rented beach house—all of us tan, my father looking like the athlete he was, with a swimmer's broad shoulders and lean torso. Other photographs, going back even further, show my mother in shorts and a sleeveless shirt, sitting on the grass with me—a chubby toddler with wide, curious eyes. My mother wore no makeup, she was freckled from the sun, and her legs were strong and smooth. She looked girlish, casual, and happy. In that photograph, we will always be younger, it will always be summer, and we will always have miles of time stretching out ahead of us.

As if carrying through with a theme, my mother and I did a photo session for a *Newsweek* piece that—it was agreed—would focus on family reconciliation more than my father's illness. We sat on the lawn, smiled, embraced, played with the dog, and added another chapter to the photographic record of our lives.

Watching our parents get older is both sad and sweet. We find ourselves frightened but awestruck at the richness of the experience, at the way our hearts soften, grow larger, absorb the truth of their mortality and our own. We have trouble separating the spiritual and the physical, and at a certain point, we stop trying, because they become the same thing.

Walking behind my father on the brick path leading from the pool up to the house, I looked at the curve of his back, the way his hand held on to the wrought-iron railing for support, and I felt my heart bruise, and then give in. The image of him younger seemed so close, but he is older now—more frail, this man who once lifted me over his head. My hand reached out to touch him, letting him know I was there. He was wearing a sweater, even though the day was warm. I felt the heat of the afternoon sun crawl up over my back, my shoulders, as we moved slowly up the path. I felt it beneath my hand that was pressed gently into my father's back, but I knew he probably didn't feel the sun's warmth. He gets cold easily now. On chilly winter days at the ranch, he used to ride in his shirtsleeves, impervious to the cold and the wind that would slice at us on high hilltops.

That afternoon, with my father ahead of me, I saw how time narrows us. His back used to be wide and sturdy; I would jump on it when I was a child, as if it were a mountain I could scramble up. His arms have, over a lifetime, lifted me into jeeps, onto horses; now he often rests his arm in mine when we walk—for reassurance, support.


MY FATHER USED TO BE the storyteller—from fables to memories of his past, storytelling was his domain. Now my mother has had to take over. She told us about the goats they used to have at the ranch. Michael and Maureen remembered; the goats were gone by the time I was born. Their two female goats gave birth to four babies each—a record, they were told. According to some almanac or someone who knew about farm animals, goats normally have only one or two offspring at a time. Since a new record for goat births had been set, my parents were invited to appear on *The Art Linkletter Show,* along with their impressive brood.

"You and Dad went on *The Art Linkletter Show* with your goats?" I asked, imagining my mother and father trying to control a group of goats on a television show.

"Yes—all eight babies and the two females," my mother said. "They were very happy to have us come, and very happy to see us leave. The goats did their business all over the studio."

But interspersed between the humorous stories and memories was more somber talk—funeral plans and how to handle the descent of the media when the time comes. Chaos will be an inevitable part of it. There will be logistical problems and an enormous need to depend on people who have a history with my parents, who can be trusted and who don't need to ask a lot of questions. Figuring out how to grieve in the midst of it all is a lesson we will learn together.

The second day I was there, when I left my parents' house in the evening to go back to the beach hotel which has become my second home, I hugged each of them goodbye and said, "I love you." Driving away, I thought about the fact that I now end every visit, every phone call, with those words. When I was a child, my father explained that the reason he and my mother always embraced and said "I love you" before parting even for a brief time was that life is unpredictable. You never know what will happen, or when your last moment will come, he told me. In case his last moments were being played out, in case his last words were being uttered, he wanted those words to be "I love you."

It didn't seem a dark or somber thought to me, and doesn't now. It's practical; it's being attentive to the mysteries of life and the emotions of those you love. It's being willing to lead with your heart, and leave a small piece of it behind.

My mother told me she picked up my book *Angels Don't Die* again and began rereading it. She suggested that maybe I should do the same. "There are things you forget in it," she said. "Valuable things that you need to read again." It's exactly what I had envisioned for that book— people opening it occasionally, reacquainting themselves with the lessons of faith that are in its pages. It also occurred to me that my mother might have read my mind; I had been thinking lately that I should reread my own book, bolster up my faith, remind myself what I've been taught about the guidance of God's hand.

Leaving my parents' house on another day, I thought about what I'm learning from my mother by being around her now—now that I'm more observant, more watchful, more open to who she is. I'm learning a dignity, a quiet power that assesses, weighs options, thinks before acting. My mother doesn't give quick answers these days; she thinks things through first. But more important, she makes me feel that all things are possible—from huge career successes to finding the right apartment, a nagging reality in my life right now, since my lease is up in a couple of months. I do need to read my own book again, but I also need to replay in my head my mother's saying that everything will work out fine.

WHILE I WAS IN Los Angeles, I was on *The Late Late Show with Tom Snyder,* and the next day I brought a tape of it to my parents' house. Something about watching it with my father hit me so deeply, I had to fight back tears. He was watching it intently, quietly, listening to me talk about the spiritual lessons he had imparted to me. I wanted desperately to probe his thoughts—it seemed that so much was going on—but I didn't want to seem as if I were interrogating him. I don't know what exactly it was that made tears well up; I only know they did. I let a lot of things go unquestioned these days.

Part of me was still a small girl, wanting my father's smile of approval, the expression he wore when I got it right, whether it was riding a wave or orchestrating perfect dressage movements on a horse. The way he would look up from a drawing I brought him—I used to draw hands, occasionally faces—was a look that would carry me through the rest of the day and beyond. I felt like I could do anything then—paint the Sistine Chapel if the chance arose. Decades later, after so much of our lives had been lived, after we went wrong in so many ways, I was sitting in my parents' bedroom with my father watching me on television. I imagined that, deep behind his silence, his intent gaze, was the look that I craved as a child. I told myself that he was thinking, She finally got it right—grew up, stopped being so angry. He was always so confused by my anger, my unfocused rage; the most content of men, he couldn't understand why he hadn't been able to impart that to me. Maybe that's what he was thinking, I decided—I really did get through to her.

Another story that came tumbling out on this visit: When my father wasn't getting much acting work and times were lean for my parents, he used to take the change from his pockets at the end of the day and put it in a box for me—the baby they had just had. He planned to do that for years until he had saved an impressive amount of money. But the cleaning lady who occasionally came in stole it. It wasn't much, but it was for me, his baby daughter. He was upset at the loss, but more upset at the fact that she would actually steal from their home.

## AUGUST 1995

When I got back to New York, I felt weighed down by the convergence of things in my life—my father, this waiting game that the whole country seems to be part of (the networks are already putting together obituary pieces about him), and finding a new apartment.

"I can't believe I put myself in a position of having to move again," I told my mother. "This will be the fifth move in two years." But as I said it, I realized it would be the first one that my mother would be part of, at least in terms of emotional support, sympathy for the tediousness of it, excitement over what I hope will be a better place. Two years ago, I moved across the country, from California to Connecticut; I lived in two houses in Connecticut, trying to fit into a town where I clearly did not belong. Desperate to move into Manhattan, I took an apartment with only a year's lease available. The year is almost up. "It will work out," my mother told me. "You'll find something better. You don't even like that apartment." Which is true.

She told me she got the pictures back that we took for *Newsweek,* and she noticed that her smile was different now, more reserved. "There is a sadness in my eyes," she said.

"We've all changed," I answered. "We all look a little different." I didn't tell her, though, that I've had trouble remembering what my eyes used to look like. I know they sparkled more, were more alive, alert, not turned inward, but I haven't been able to recapture the image. An interviewer once said to me that America lost its innocence when President Kennedy was shot. Maybe we lose some innocence in saying goodbye to our parents. Part of us goes with them—the part that can never be a child again. Something else is lost when we say goodbye to a lover, a partner—we wonder if we will ever love again, ever look ahead with as much hope as we once had. Our eyes show all of it—the loss, the fear, the growing up.

In a taxi today, driving along the West Side Highway, I suddenly envisioned a world without Ronald Reagan. Politics are irrelevant in this—he's been a strong heartbeat in this country and in the world. I felt the silencing of his heartbeat, the hush that will be left behind when he's gone. I reached for my sunglasses to cover the tears.

THE SPIRITUAL TEACHER Jiddu Krishnamurti said in order to give the deepest comfort to one who is dying, we need to let him know that in his death a part of us will die as well and will go with him. He will be assured then that he won't be alone.

There will be parts of me, I know, that will go with my father—travel with him, keep him company on the river crossing we call death. The child who stood beside him in the ocean, holding his hand and squealing when a fish swam between her legs—she will clutch his hand again, face the waves, and head into deep water, trusting that if he is with her, she won't drown. And the girl riding behind him on horseback, galloping up hills and along leafy trails, who still goes on those rides in the green eternity of memory—she will ride behind him again, turn down whatever trail he chooses. The teenager whose anger blinded her to the sadness in her father's eyes will soften and take his arm. The woman who is now trying to crowd a lifetime of memories into an embrace, a meeting of eyes, the words "I love you"—part of her will follow him into the vastness of a world beyond this one, trusting that in death there is also birth.

After a California wildfire destroyed much of our ranch in the early sixties, my father showed me from horseback the green shoots and new growth peeking out of the soil just a few months later. He was wise enough to know that life lessons are as close as the earth beneath our feet. I hold that in my mind these days, imagine parts of myself growing back, green and new, replacing the parts I will gladly send with my father when he is ready to leave.

The only thing to do in New York in August is flee from the city. The heat is stifling; the air doesn't move; trees and people wilt.

"This is the kind of weather that can turn entire families into mass murderers," I said to my friend who was generous enough to invite me to his house on Fire Island for the weekend.

We were in his car, the air conditioner on high, escaping from the city to the ferry which would take us to the Pines—no cars; long, lazy days on the beach; late dinners and late mornings. I will return to the task of moving into my new apartment, where I will finally be able to see the sky. It's twelve floors up, with double-height windows in the living room, a view of Lincoln Center, and a glimpse of the river. It's bright and cheerful, unlike the dark cave I've been living in for a year.

From the first time I went to Fire Island, I thought of it as a comfort zone. There is an emotional tapestry there that I understand; people are friendly, are there to have fun, but there is a shared sadness floating beneath the surface. It requires no explanations, no apologies; it's just there. Everyone who goes to the island has, in one way or another, been touched by AIDS, and therefore by grief. Grieving is a learned art; it doesn't get easier, but it does get smoother. You learn the pathways through it and around it. You learn to laugh and have fun even in the midst of pain. These are the survival skills.

One evening, two men were talking about a mutual friend who now has full-blown AIDS and dementia.

"Did you hear what he did?" one of them said. "He bought a couple of Cadillacs and went around telling everyone he was going to drive them to Cuba and give them to Castro as gifts."

Against a backdrop of laughter, the other man said, "Doing his part for world peace, huh?"

Laughter salves the wound of losing someone you love; my mother and I have discovered that. And on this small island, the roster of summer visitors has changed dramatically during the past decade. Over the weekend, pink umbrellas were put out on the beach—hundreds of them—as a statement of AIDS awareness. To advertise a charity AIDS event, foldout announcements were dropped off at each house; the list of names was staggering—

people who are memories now. The friend whom I stayed with knew eighty-five of the men listed.

On the ferry coming over to the island, I noticed a man with telltale purple blotches on his neck, a few others who were painfully thin, and I remembered a gay man saying to me years ago, "My friends are divided now between who is positive and who is negative."

Sunday morning, I walked along the beach and ran into a man I knew from my two visits to the island. He's tan, muscular. But I saw it in his eyes—a shadow, like a cloud floating across the sun. "He's been positive for about eight years," my friend told me. "He's doing well now— last summer he was quite sick."

Death is always nearby here, lurking in blood-streams, taking friends away. It strolls along the shore and gives no indication that it will drift off anytime soon. I feel more at home here because there is a shadow in my eyes, too. As my father retreats, part of me dies. I know that part will come back, be reborn—be stronger—but for now it's just another kind of dying. In the city, I often feel out of place, self-conscious about the sadness I carry around with me—the shadow that I know will get darker before it lifts. On Fire Island, I don't have to apologize for it or even explain. My head feels lighter here, clearer.

The *Tibetan Book of Living and Dying* says that because our consciousness is mounted on a "wind" it needs an aperture through which to leave the body. If, at death, it leaves through the crown of the head, we are reborn into a pure land where we can proceed toward enlightenment. I thought of that as I walked on the beach, with the heat bearing down and the afternoon breeze still somewhere out at sea. I thought of leaving room in my thoughts and my heart—for wind, for hope, for a glimpse of an easier time for all of us.

I WAS TALKING WITH someone at an afternoon party on Sunday. A film of clouds had drifted across the sky, the sun looked milky, and there was some relief from the heat. He looked around at the mostly male gathering and said, "You know, you always wonder these days who will be next, who won't be here by next summer. It's terrible to think like that, but it's unavoidable. I've lost so many friends."

It's a somber way of marking time; my family does it, too, and he's right—it is unavoidable. "Maybe we just have to try to make friends with death," I suggested. "Maybe that's the challenge. It's better than suffering." I noticed as I said it a man walking onto the deck, winded and very weak. Someone led him to a chair.

"But no one has prepared us for this," the man I was talking to answered. "We're young and we're watching our friends die. Our parents, their parents, had time to prepare themselves. For the most part, old age was what brought disease and the need for caregiving. We sit beside friends who are in their thirties and forties, watching them die."

"But when death comes, doesn't it seem kind at that point?" I asked. I thought he must know more about grieving than I do—he's done it more.

"Maybe. But we're still losing them. They're not here, and they never got to live out their lives."

We are the generation who couldn't conceive of

thirty, who thought we'd never get old, who wanted to burn out before that dreaded stage of life. Now we're burying our own. They die too young, and we feel old before our time. This man was right—no one prepared us. It's become a rite of passage—for all of us—sitting at bedsides, waiting for the next disconnected phone number, the next funeral service. It's as if everything has sped up. Grief doesn't wait for us to get older; death isn't something hovering in the distance. We have to think about it, and talk about it. We have no choice.

I choose to try to make friends with death, dress it in something more colorful than basic black. Sometimes I think of it not as a single entity, but as a band of angels, dressed in soft shades of blue and white. The other night, in that limbo state between sleep and dreams, I saw my father being lifted up by four angels. They were gentle, delicate creatures, and they carried him above this troubled world and the disease that's been claiming him by increments. He was looking down—to my mother, smiling at her, with both sadness and love in his eyes.

I sweeten the image of death—remove the cloak, the shroud. I give it a serene, kind face, one which understands sorrow. I need to, because without the intervention of death, this disease will march on, conquering all of my father, leaving just the outline of him.

I try to forget the stories about Alzheimer's that well-meaning people share with me, but of course I can't. A friend who as a child adored his uncle recently had to put him into an institution for Alzheimer's patients. Two days later, the uncle who used to take him fishing and camping tried to smother another patient with a pillow. He was stopped before the woman died and, five minutes later, had no memory of what he'd done. Someone else told me about a relative who passed through the stages of Alzheimer's to end up locked in a relentless rage, which she acted out on her loved ones—except she didn't recall them as loved ones. To her, they were just people in her way. These stories make me think of death as the garden gate my father needs to pass through to be at peace.

Shortly after my father's diagnosis, I said to my brother Ron, "We're losing our father—how do you feel about this?" "It's different for me than it is for you," he said, with male stoicism. "It's a little easier for me, I think. I'm more complete in my relationship with him—I didn't need his love as desperately as you did."

I didn't press further, because I had doubts about the completeness. We are never complete with losing someone who has been melded to us through birth, or love, or both. But maybe hungry love is unique to fathers and daughters; maybe sons always hold something back. Still, only love can ravage us, break us in pieces, then put us back together again. At some point, I sifted through the rubble and discovered who I was: I am my father's daughter. I have his off-kilter smile, his long legs and wide shoulders. At moments, I have his humor. It seemed such a simple truth, yet I had run away from it with such fury for so much of my life. I will never wish that I had needed him less, never regret the years I hungered to know him, to understand who he was, even as I ran away from the part of him that lived in me.

I needed to run away in order to come home. I returned in time to say goodbye to my father and to watch my mother be transformed by a sorrow which she feels is dismantling her but which is actually making her more beautiful. I returned to hear my sister, Maureen's, voice break when she said to me, "I'm going to miss him so much."

If sons lose fathers differently than daughters do, it's only in the way they handle the pain. My brother Michael puts on a brave face; Ron turns philosophical. Maureen and I reach for sunglasses when tears well up—we wait until we're alone to cry. But underneath is the same truth for all of us: we will be without a father soon. In some ways, we already are. We will delve into our memories to touch him again, to hear his voice, to keep alive the years we had with him.

## SEPTEMBER 1995

My father taught all of his children to ride a bicycle, and he taught us the same way. After the training wheels came off, he would run behind us, holding on to the back of the seat so we would feel secure. One day, without our realizing it, he would let go. I remember looking back, expecting to see him with his hands on the bike, and seeing only the distance I had traveled without him—a ribbon of road behind me, my father standing where he had left me, waving and smiling.

There are memories I have in common with my siblings—childhood memories—but our lives branched off as we grew older. There is an age difference between us. Maureen and Michael are roughly a decade older than I; Ron is six years younger. Each of them grew up just outside the flames of the sixties and early seventies—either before the flames ignited or after they had been quelled. I was branded by them.

My generation has now stumbled into its own legacy. We have looked behind us at the broken cords, the frayed ends, but we have noticed something else: some cords didn't break. We are bound to those who went before us, to the parents who gave birth to us and the ancestors whom we will never know, despite all our efforts to cut ourselves free. And now, finally, we are old enough to handle those cords with more loving hands, to follow them back, knowing they will lead us to parts of ourselves that were once lost.

No generation in history struggled against its parents as much as the baby boomers—breast-fed on the blandness of the fifties, set on fire by the renaissance of the sixties. Now we're in our forties. We're calmer, wiser, our vision is clearer, and we're losing our parents.

Because we struggled so hard, ran so fast, we have a longer journey back. We have miles to travel before we can soften our hearts to the experience of saying goodbye to our mothers and fathers. Those of us who blazed a path through the sixties may have been part of a revolution, but we forgot to unshackle our hearts. It's our hearts now that are being invited, by the aging of our parents, to open wider than they ever have before, to return to the innocence and love that we knew before we discovered the drug-rush of anger.

Some of us have made the return journey. Our feet are bloodied, but our hearts are in better shape. I think sometimes of how different my life would be if my parents hadn't lived this long, or if I hadn't listened to the echo of my own despair. The thought comes to me in small moments—walking with my father, my arm through his. What if he weren't there to touch, and I had to live my life with only the remnants of my anger at my fingertips? It comes to me with the sound of my mother's voice and the things I am learning from her now. I might have been too late. I might have been left with only silence and distance.

There is a loneliness to grief that is inescapable. You lie awake at night and feel it tunnel through your heart. I walk through my days carrying a weight inside me. But it's a shared weight. There are things my mother and I say only to each other, experiences no one else will hear about. It would have been unbearable to lose my father without my family, without the daily phone conversations with my mother. I cringe when friends tell me that their parents are old and they haven't spoken to them in years. Once that felt like home to me; now it seems like a place I visited, a long time ago, when I didn't know better.

For much of the eighties, I saved my silence for my parents and set my most defiant voice loose for the country to hear. I didn't agree with my father's politics or policies, and I was relentlessly vocal about it. A woman friend of mine who is my age said, "It was inevitable that someone from our generation would represent the anger that a lot of us felt. It had to happen. In a sense, you were the archetype for our generation—the angry daughter railing against her father. Of course, your father also happened to be president."

"Great," I answered. "I'm so happy to have been able to fulfill that role."

On several occasions my father asked me to come talk with him, listen to his viewpoints. My response was that I already knew. I shudder at that now. What did it matter if I already knew his point of view? He was asking for communication, and I rejected him, hurt his feelings; I thought I was working for disarmament and a more peaceful world. The arsenal of nuclear weapons was indeed dangerous and terrifying, but so were the armaments of a generation that didn't understand how deadly its anger was.

In 1982, there was a huge antinuclear rally at the

Rose Bowl in Pasadena. It lasted all day and into the night and featured some of the biggest names in music and Hollywood. Thousands of people were in the audience. Looking back now, I can see so clearly that there were other ways of showing my ideological support; I could have written a statement and had someone read it, or put out something in the press saying that I supported the antinuclear movement but didn't want to oppose my father in a personal way by showing up at a demonstration. But this was my naïveté: I didn't see how personal my presence there was. "Why can't I be here just like everyone else?" was my thinking. But the truth was, I wasn't like anyone else. No one else at that entire event, either in the audience or appearing on the stage, had a parent in the White House. By showing up and walking onstage, all I was really saying was that I was locked in battle with my parents. On "Peace Sunday," I was waging war.

Jesse Jackson spoke before me and launched into a personal attack on my father, closing his speech by leading the entire stadium in a chant of "Get a new president." This is what I remember as I stood offstage: The look on the face of one of my Secret Service agents, a look that said he was waiting for me to leave, cancel my plans to speak, a look that was telling me I should. And an awful cold dread swelling up inside me, even though the day was sweltering. Jesse Colin Young came on right after Reverend Jackson, right before me; I remember him singing "Imagine"; I told myself that the song would diffuse the hostility that had been whipped up. My motive was not to attack my father personally, but motives don't stick in people's minds—appearances do. I felt sick when I walked onstage, but I told myself it was just nerves. I gave my short speech; I spoke about peace, about making the world less dangerous. And I felt it—in the applause, in the way people were listening to me—the irrelevance of my words. My appearance that day was what spoke to them, and it wasn't the message I had wanted to impart. Years later, I met a man who was there, and he said, "My first thought, when you came on after what Jesse Jackson had done, was, She really must hate her father."

My manager at the time went to Reverend Jackson and asked how he could have been so inconsiderate as to start up that chant, knowing I was coming on after him. He said, "If she can't take it, she shouldn't be here."

For years after that, I blamed Jesse Jackson. Now I think his curt reply was correct. The best thing I could have done for world peace that day was stay home.

Time and disease have conspired to leave me with words I will never be able to say to my father. I want to apologize, explain to him that in my heart I wanted to be a conduit between his conservatism and the antinuclear movement, which I sincerely believed in. But the wishes of my heart competed with my arrogance and my youth; my heart didn't stand a chance. I want to tell him that I wish I had accepted his invitation to talk. I wish I had listened to him—not because I think anyone's viewpoints would have changed, but because listening is a loving thing to do, and because he deserved that much from me. I can only have this conversation in my imagination, and often I do. I imagine his eyes shining, his head cocked to one side, the way it did when he was paying attention to what someone was telling him. I imagine him smiling, saying something like, I wish it had been different, too.

His head doesn't tilt to one side now; his eyes frequently look beyond us. We have moved past the turmoil of those years, the rigid silences. But my penance is the words left unsaid.

Secretly, I have always envied my siblings for the fact that their politics didn't clash with our father's as much as mine did. It made their lives more harmonious. The dissonance in mine haunted me, and still does.

Maureen has always been essentially conservative—a committed Republican. Whatever small disagreements she and our father had over specific issues, they had in common the architecture of a conservative ideology. She had a bond with him where I had an open wound. I was wrenched apart by our disagreements; I was unable to close that chasm between us. If only he were a liberal Democrat, I would think, or if I could truly embrace a Republican point of view. Both of these fantasies were impossible. Ronald Reagan seemed born to represent conservatism; his beliefs were sincere and deeply held. I was incapable of lowering the flame on my liberal opinions. They were hot-blooded, passionate, and always seemed to be singeing somebody.

My brother Ron found a middle ground—some sort of demilitarized zone of his own making. His politics were, at their core level, more liberal than our father's, but there were some conservative views thrown into the mix. He could discuss issues dispassionately, logically. To him, the political was not personal.

Michael has established a career as a conservative radio host. His credentials in the Republican Party have never been questioned.

I've wished so often that my beliefs were smaller,

more malleable, of a more moderate temperature. Years ago, I used to wish that my parents were right when they said I had been influenced by the left-wing radicals of my generation—the fiery evangelists of the sixties who took over Haight-Ashbury, brought chaos to Berkeley, and raised their fists in the spirit of revolution. It would be so easy if I could chalk it up to peer pressure. But I can't.

I have regrets over the ways in which I expressed my political beliefs, but the beliefs themselves have never changed. Now, years after my father left office, when he is unable to entertain a political discussion, or even perhaps to care about such things, our differences still feel like a chasm to me, a gap that will never be closed.

So I choose to back away from the chasm and walk in the other direction. I choose to just be his daughter. I want the feeling of being small, running toward him, knowing his arms will catch me, lift me high in the air. I want him to melt away my anger or my grumpiness by telling me to look deep into his eyes and "Whatever you do, don't laugh." Within seconds, my anger would splinter into laughter. I want nothing more than to be his daughter again, without the wrench of political disagreements. When I read articles criticizing the policies of the Reagan years, but lauding Ronald Reagan as a man, my emotions collide, refuse to fall into any kind of order. I don't know what to do with those feelings. I never will.


MY MOTHER'S VOICE is usually a barometer of how tired she is; frequently, it sags from exhaustion and sorrow. We are all caught up in this waiting game; we expect the desolation to begin, and then we realize it already has. It's audible in our voices, but it's most obvious in my mother's.

Sometimes she and I talk euphemistically about the end. We use phrases like "when this is over" or short, self-conscious words like "afterward." Other times, we talk clinically, stripping things down to bare wood. It's as if, at moments, we are speaking directly to death, staring it down. We don't blink or mince words. We talk about what life might be like after my father dies. But always our voices have a leaden quality to them, a heaviness, as if an anchor were tied to us.

I grasp the moments when my mother's voice lightens. I search for the ingredients of this change, try to manufacture or duplicate them.

Twice this week I've heard her voice lift—wing through the phone line sounding younger, more hopeful. A friend of hers told her a story about a man he knew from AA meetings. The story was about a miracle, a phenomenon that couldn't be explained rationally, and she couldn't wait to tell me.

"The man had gone to George Washington Hospital," she said, reminding me that it was the hospital my father was rushed to when he was shot. "This man was in the examining room, and for some reason, which he still can't explain, he got a piece of paper and a pen, went over to a piece of medical equipment, and did a tracing. After a few seconds, what showed up was a crucifix. He was embarrassed to tell the story because he thought people might assume he was crazy."

"It doesn't sound crazy to me," I said.

"Isn't it an incredible story?" my mother asked. Clearly, craziness was not her assessment either.

I was listening to something beyond the story itself—I was listening to the melody of my mother's voice, the energy that was humming through it. She had gotten a glimpse of a miracle—someone else's, but that didn't matter.

The other occasion was an offer which came unexpectedly.

"You're not going to believe this," she said, her voice girlish and light. "I got offered a movie role. I thought it was a joke at first."

I assumed it was a cameo. We were both wrong. It was neither a joke nor a cameo role; it was a serious offer to costar with Albert Brooks in a feature film, playing his mother.

"If it were sometime later," my mother told me, "I could probably do it. It's just the timing. There's no way I can do something like that right now. But it's the most wonderful script and a great role. When I was under contract to MGM I used to beg them to let me do a comedy, but they never would. They always had me pregnant and in the kitchen."

"You know what this is?" I said. "It's a way of showing you what's possible, what opportunities are open to you. Things you never even thought of will present themselves to you. After everything is over, something else will come along—maybe even this. Films get delayed all the time."

These moments in my mother's life lighten me as well. My day is a bit calmer, a bit more content. I feel more hopeful, less afraid for her.

A friend of hers said that, despite what she's going through, she looks well—lovely, in fact. She was puzzled by the comment—flattered, but puzzled.

"Don't you know what he meant, though?" I asked her. "You're going through a painful, difficult time, but you're allowing it to deepen you, soften you. There's great beauty in that, and it shows up as physical beauty. People who have gone through pain and surrendered to the experience have a loveliness to them."

I've noticed it in my mother also. I should have mentioned it to her before, I thought, when I hung up the phone, and went to the mirror to scrutinize my own face. I'm not a good judge of my appearance; I tend to berate what I see in the mirror. But I forced myself to set my judgments aside and envision the changes I want to see. I cautioned my face to not turn hard or bitter. I asked my eyes to not become wintry and chilly to those around me. If I can let grief, and change, and the mystery of this drawn-out parting from my father, flood me—erase boundaries and hard edges—it will show outwardly.

I F   I   C O U L D   be a time of day, I would choose to be twilight. It's soft and painted with different colors—blues, lavenders, grays. It's been called the hour of sorrow, but there is a quiet, imperial beauty to it. It ushers in stars and doesn't mind leaving when its short time is up. It bends into night—willingly, graciously—like a woman who has known great sorrow and is more lovely because of it. I usually talk to my mother at twilight.

The same time *Angels Don't Die* came out, a book of quotes from my father was also published. I found a quote in it that struck me, from the 1988 Republican National Convention:

> There's still a lot of brush to clear out at the ranch, fences that need repair, and horses to ride. But I want you to know that if the fires ever dim, I'll leave my phone number and address behind just in case you need a foot soldier. Just let me know, and I'll be there, as long as words don't leave me and as long as this sweet country strives to be special during its shining moment on earth.

We plan our lives, envision them, relax into our hopes. But nothing is ever certain. I know my parents thought their life would settle into a more peaceful one—more private, with some ventures into the public arena. My father's love for this nation made him willing to step into the spotlight again if he felt it was necessary. The line that saddens me the most is "as long as words don't leave me."

I suppose none of us know how we will grow silent, slip away from this life—or when. It happens in God's time, not ours, and we grow quiet. My father watches more, talks less, these days. The world will remember his voice; my family will also remember his silence. Clear and powerful, it's the sound of someone leaving us.

## October 1995

Another of my mother's friends has died—suddenly, unexpectedly. His heart just stopped, refused to go on. By the time he was rushed to the hospital, he was gone. For his funeral service, my mother picked white roses from her garden and set them on his coffin—a gift from the earth. When I was a child, she was always clipping roses and bringing them into the house, arranging them in vases. I picture her now, picking them for a sadder purpose, bending over her friend's coffin with her offering of white roses, saying another goodbye.

After I hung up the phone from this conversation, I thought about the heart—the physical one with all its strength and fragility, and the emotional one—the troubadour that sings us into love, and danger, and deep friendships. I thought of how some hearts yearn for harbors, anchor there, and how some keep heading out to sea. My mother's heart has nourished itself in the harbor of marriage and family—firmly anchored, with no ear for siren songs. Mine has been a stubborn sailor's heart—tougher physically than emotionally. It muscled its way through reckless years of too much youth, too many drugs, and now endures the miles I want to run, the weights I insist on lifting, the brutal workouts I'm somewhat addicted to.

But love or the hint of it has sent it on watery blue journeys. I think about its wanderlust and long for some of what my mother has known. Harbors don't frighten me as much as they used to.

My father's heart has a strange rhythm to it—irregular, shocking to any doctor who listens to it for the first time. But it's a stoic heart, one that valiantly got him through afternoons of bodysurfing in rough waves and long days of chopping wood, riding horses, clearing trails at the ranch. A heart that kept beating while surgeons' hands rummaged in his chest, searching for a bullet that they finally found less than an inch from its chambers. It's done what my father has asked of it—beat on steadily, with its own crazy rhythm. He didn't worry about it, and it didn't trouble him. When the time comes, it will just stop.

My parents' hearts fell in love and brought mine into the world—I have a reverence for this which I didn't have before. Death makes you think of birth, and further back—to conception, the singular act that calls forth a life. Genes are strung together, necklaces of DNA—characteristics that parents recognize and children question. Parents stare at their babies, searching for pieces of themselves. Usually, they find them—the eyes, the shape of the mouth, the jaw line.

But who knows which genes blink on at conception, at birth, or sometime after? I grew up on the lullaby of my father's language. It transported me to a land of endless stories. From the time of my earliest memory, I hung on to his words. He wove them into ropes, and I dangled there, waiting for him to pull me up into another adventure. I don't know when I fell in love with the idea of weaving words together myself, only that I did. Writing became my lifeline, something beyond choice, something vital, but at times destructive. In the past, I've used it to wound my parents, sharpening my words and aiming them at the people who, by their union, linked up the genes that turned me into a writer.

Some would say it's ironic that my mother is now hanging on to my writing, a lifeline of sorts for her, a guarantee that this story we are living now will be told truthfully, but gently. My father, if he could, would probably just say it was a long time in coming.

OFTEN, MY MOTHER AND I share other people's words—letters and cards sent to us from strangers whom we may never meet. Sometimes we receive poems or stories from the lives of people we will never meet.

Sharing them is how we fortify each other these days.

My mother reminded me that when I was younger, I used to copy poems for my parents and give them as gifts on their anniversary or on birthdays. She recalled that when she would pick me up at school, I wouldn't be playing with the other children; I would be sitting on a bench reading. She told a friend during my childhood that she knew I would someday be a writer.

Maya Angelou said that love is a bridge, where one person crosses over to another. I wrote down her words because I felt they described the heart of the story I'm trying to tell. We are learning to build a bridge over the chaos of life, the deep waters of our own history together, and ultimately over the pain of losing my father.

With Alzheimer's, the person afflicted with the disease retreats, becomes enveloped in a foggy realm that leaves loved ones outside. But there is no retreat for my mother. She's left with the loneliness, the pain of a life that's changing around her—narrowing, becoming more solitary. It must feel to her like the moon and stars have shut their eyes, turning the world darker.

"There are good days and bad days," she says when people ask. It seems an obvious statement, but it works to keep people's curiosity at arm's length. But for anyone who has lived through it, the bad days start to pull on the good ones, unraveling the seams of everything that once seemed secure. Often, when talking to my mother, I feel fear and sorrow twist together inside me, like serpents coiling around each other, forming what I have come to imagine is the shape of grief. I apologized to her for not being able to fly out to L.A. this month; the expense and the busywork of moving has made it impossible. Even though she understands and we will be together in New York during the month, I feel terrible about it. I was absentmindedly drawing on a yellow pad—it looked like storm clouds. An appropriate image.

We find our way past this gathering of storm clouds by focusing on lighter subjects sometimes; at the moment, it's my new apartment. I've described it to my mother, but she'll be here in a few days and will finally get to see it for herself. I haven't actually moved in yet. I'm going through the messy, transformational stages of having walls painted, closets redone; in the meantime, I'm carrying things over box by box. Yesterday evening, I went over to watch the sunset, which is impossible to see from the apartment I have been living in. My writing room will be a loft above the living room—the city version of a tree house. Fixing up my apartment has given my mother and me something to get excited about, but it's more than that. She'll be part of the evolution of my home, just as she has become part of the evolution of my life.

There is a theory that our homes are extensions of ourselves; our deepest currents can be traced by examining the physical environment we call home. It is why, someone once told me, you have to be careful whom you let through your front door. You are also letting them into your life in a significant, vulnerable way. For decades, I kept my mother out of my home, out of my life. My illusion was that I was also keeping her out of my heart. But our parents cannot be banished from our hearts—we are tied to them with cords we barely understand. We can close our eyes, pretend the cords don't exist, but we can't cut them. They span time and generations, bind us together through the angriest years, the deepest heartaches, through silence and distance, and eventually they reel us in and carry us home.

I happened to see a television interview with Maya Angelou, and she mentioned Thomas Wolfe's title *You Can't Go Home Again;* she said that, as much as she admires his work, she disagrees with that particular sentiment. She said what seems more true is that you can never really leave home. That's the truth that finally caught up with me. I ran hard and fast, thinking I was running away from home, but I was running in a circle, wearing myself out. I began to grow up when I stopped, opened my arms, my heart, my life, to my parents—when I acknowledged the cords between us that had stretched for miles without breaking.

THE DAY I TOOK my mother to see my new apartment happened to be the day of O. J. Simpson's not-guilty verdict. She and I watched the verdict together and then walked down Central Park West—numb, a little shell-shocked—to see where I would soon be living.

Our mood changed the minute we walked through the front door. The drama of this apartment is the airiness, the light, the high ceilings that make claustrophobia impossible.

"I'm so happy for you," my mother said, hugging me.

We talked about how I was going to decorate it, where to put the couch. It was early afternoon, but the day had already catapulted us through a wide array of emotions—shock to excitement, sadness to joy. It struck me that we would remember the day for that—for all its changes. The world sweeps us up in events beyond our control, yet our own lives rumble on as well. The times when both seem to collide and intertwine are particularly memorable, and we're forever bonded to the people who share them with us.

By the time my mother returns to New York, later in the month, I'll be moved in, probably surrounded by chaos and decorating dilemmas, but by less clutter. I watch myself weeding out the excess among the things I own—even furniture—and I think it's a metaphor for how I'm changing internally. It's partly, I suppose, the effect of watching my father's life ebb. I've become acutely aware of the slippage of time. It does go quickly—it's startling the first time that realization really takes hold. I don't want my heart to be cluttered with trivial dramas and indulgences, nor do I want my home to be cluttered with "stuff."

"The eye needs to rest," my mother said when we were standing in my new apartment, visualizing where things should go. She was talking about interior decorating, but I thought about it metaphorically as well. It's in the blank spaces, the gaps, that clarity comes to us, and, if we're lucky, peace of mind.

I WENT WITH HER to a dinner given by friends of hers, and I carefully watched her response when she was asked about my father. Her answer has changed a bit, as has mine. She averted her eyes and said, "Well, the disease is what it is." I've changed what used to be my stock answer to the question "How is your father?" I can no longer say, "Fine." I think my eyes would give me away. I've settled on a nonanswer. "It's a challenging time for all of us, but we're coping." I say it and turn my eyes away, hoping that people won't press further. Usually, they don't.

The irony of living a public life is that the areas which are deemed private are kept so by carving them out with excruciating exactitude—by surveying the landscape with a keen eye. Even the closest friends are not given complete information; details are withheld. These private domains become fortresses, citadels that are guarded militantly, stoically. You alter your outward persona to protect the inner sanctum—the raw truth of the life you're really living.

And sometimes you alter your own awareness of the truth. I spoke to my father on the phone the other evening—briefly, to say goodnight to him, to say I love you. His voice sounded strong and certain, and I let myself imagine that there is no disease marshaling its forces in his brain, conquering him slowly. I imagined him remembering the phone call days later and smiling; it may or may not happen that way—I needed to suspend reality for a few hours, color it the way I wanted.

Already the world is acknowledging the silence of my father's voice. My mother has been asked to speak at the Republican convention. "You're his voice now," she was told. When she and I talked about this, we didn't talk politics. We discussed the mean-spiritedness of the '92 convention and the fact that she wouldn't want to lend my father's name to a repeat performance of the same invective. So no decision was made. "Maybe if Colin Powell runs," she said, leaving it at that for the moment.

## LATE OCTOBER 1995

It rained on my birthday—a relentless, torrential storm that was particularly dramatic outside the high windows of my new home. My mother and I spent most of the day together. We had lunch in my apartment, spanned a conversational continent—from decorating, to New York gossip, to my father. The moment I will remember forever is my mother sitting on a bar chair at the wide counter that separates my kitchen from the living room, saying, "I don't know how to be alone. I've never been alone." She was fighting back tears, looking into a future that chills her with fear, as the rain flooded down outside the windows. She looked so tiny and the world—the storm—seemed so huge. I felt again the helplessness that's becoming familiar—an unwelcome companion in my life. There was nothing to say to make the moment any different than what it was. She will learn to be alone—somehow, although I don't think anyone on this earth can tell her how. It has to come from deep inside—one of those reservoirs that people don't know about until they fall off the edge of the earth they've known and some deep pool of strength saves them.

Last year, my birthday was sad, lonely—a lifetime away from what it was this year. It wasn't until after my birthday that my mother and I met at the Carlyle Hotel, changing the course of our relationship and beginning a journey that would heal our fractured family. It's strange to me to think that only a year has passed, yet so much has happened.

MY MOTHER AND I flew from New York to Washington, D.C., for a huge birthday celebration for Margaret Thatcher—black-tie, hundreds of people, mostly conservative in their political views. It's not only the type of event I would have shunned in past years, no one would have dared invite me. Now, even though I might be an unusual addition to this kind of evening, my mother and I can joke about it.

"I do know of one other liberal who will be there," I said to her. "So at least I won't be the token one."

I wondered what it would have been like during my father's administration if I'd had the same easiness with our differences, the same willingness to laugh them off.

During the cocktail hour, I stood beside my mother, and most of the people who came up to us said how happy they were to see us together. I could feel how much that meant to her, and it meant as much to me—this network of people sending us wishes and prayers. And their prayers are also for my father. His absence was felt at the Thatcher event; the two of them had a strong friendship, unusual between world leaders.

In my father's absence, it fell to my mother to address Mrs. Thatcher and the guests, extend birthday wishes from both her and my father. I knew she was nervous about it. I said a silent prayer for her when she walked up to the stage—her tears come easily, unexpectedly, these days. Behind her, large television screens were showing pictures of my father and Mrs. Thatcher—in another time, a time of more glory and less sadness. It was a blessing, I thought, that my mother couldn't see them while she was speaking—they probably would have made her cry. She got a standing ovation, and I knew that so many feelings were being played out in that room, many of them for my father and the weight of his absence. I thought of his friendship with Margaret Thatcher; the world might be more civilized, more peaceful, if world leaders could relate the way they did, regardless of their ideologies.

The last picture that was flashed onto the television screens was of my father smiling and winking. It's how I want to remember him. That wink—he still does it. It's so Irish and warm, a sign of friendship and amusement at life. I have found myself winking at him just so he'll wink back at me. When I was a child, it made me see the folly of whatever drama I had concocted. It cut through, said, You can't take life that seriously. It was like a secret password, one that always had a predictable effect, and still does. When I see my father wink, I feel better.

## NOVEMBER 1995

We are all aware of time passing quickly. The holidays are almost here, and hovering behind them is, for my family, the feeling that it might be my father's last Christmas. But there is also the ever-present state of limbo in which we find ourselves—the strange sense that time might just be standing still, stalling, lurching forward unevenly, or not at all. For someone with Alzheimer's, time becomes momentary, immediate; it loses its linear flow and becomes snagged, oftentimes in the moment at hand. Those who bear witness to that find themselves adjusting their own perceptions. My family tries to handle time as my father does—pause with him, freeze-frame the moment. I've reminded my mother at times that Einstein said the time-space continuum that we have such faith in is only a figment of our imaginations anyway. So whose perceptions are right? In my father's presence, we follow his lead, try to fit time into the image he has of it.

The other morning, he said to my mother, "I'm eighty-four." It was a comment unconnected to any other—a single thought that sprang into his mind, found its way to his voice, and hung in the air. We've all done it—been struck by the season, the years we've lived, the time we've known another person. We're hit suddenly by the brevity of life and the speed at which it travels. We say, "It's winter," and behind that is a sense that only yesterday we were putting away our winter clothes, throwing open the windows for summer. We comment on a child's mature age, yet we can still feel how that child once fit into the crook of our arm, still hear the echo of baby sounds. Recently, I said to a friend who lives in Los Angeles but was in New York doing a film, "We've known each other over fifteen years." He nodded, struck by the same thought. I knew him before he had children; he knew me before I allowed myself to have parents. The observation was singular, independent, yet part of a larger web. The sentence was perched on top of years of memories.

My father said, "I'm eighty-four," early in the morning when he and my mother had just woken up and were lying together as they have for half their lives.

When she told me about it, I wondered if he was marking time for a more somber purpose; I wondered if he was marking his exit—the age he would be when he says goodbye. I look for signs now, listen for them, because I believe that people might know when they're about to leave this earth, and they tell you in subtle ways. You have to pay attention, read between the lines, brush off the words, and look beneath them. Maybe he was bracketing his life, defining it, dating it—for himself, but more, I think, for the rest of us. He didn't elaborate on the thought. It remained solitary, mysterious, and is something that keeps tugging at me.

When you're losing someone, there are no ordinary moments. The smallest gestures, the simplest phrases, take on a larger meaning. My mother comments frequently on how sweet my father is—in the small consider-ations, the way he waits for her before walking out of a room, kisses her when he sees her even if only a few moments have passed. It isn't that she's just discovered this quality in him; it's that his sweetness has remained untouched by a disease that steals so much, and steals ran-domly, like a thief who grabs whatever he sees.

Time always steals something, I thought, when my mother said to me, "No one should get this disease." I didn't really know how to respond to her. There is so much in the world that isn't as it should be. My father would say, "God has his reasons," and he would be com-forted by his faith in God's wisdom. I'm not as consistent. There are times when I slip into the solace of faith, and I know it's a better way to live. But other times I find myself shaking my fist at the heavens, asking why, espe-cially when I think of the life I've already lived, the time I wasted, the abrupt turns down wrong roads. Why didn't a voice from heaven stop me? I often think, and then just as quickly it occurs to me that I wouldn't have listened to any voice but my own anyway.

Late tonight, I walked over to the mantel in my apartment to blow out the candles that I light whenever I'm home in the evening, because someone once told me that you can never be sad when you look into a candle flame. Other than an assortment of candles and hurricane lamps, I have on my mantel a picture of my godmother, Colleen Moore, a silent-film star who spent her later years on a ranch in northern California; a photograph of the squirrel I raised from a baby when I lived in Los Angeles—an exquisite little creature who was both tame and wild. Next to it is a Boris Vallejo print of a woman lying back on a hillside looking up at a unicorn—the picture is bold, sensual, an unapologetic fantasy. There is a photograph of my father, which was what reeled me in tonight. He is jumping his horse, years ago, at the ranch we owned when I was growing up. It's a black-and-white photograph, taken on a gray, misty day, and the photographer got him and his horse in midair, just before her front hooves came down. I moved in close to the picture, studied his horse's physique—her powerful chest muscles contracting as she cleared the jump. I could almost smell the heat of her, the sweat, feel the smoothness of her coat beneath my hands. My father's form was perfect; he was with his horse in the singular, graceful act of taking a jump. I could hear him saying, "There is nothing as good for the inside of a man as the outside of a horse." He said it often, and the echo came back to me from across the years. Wintry days at the ranch were the ones I liked the best, when the mist never quite lifted and the horses were spirited and eager to gallop.

As I stood there, I wished that the photograph could take me back, pull me into it, return me to days I know are gone. I wanted to go back with an older heart, a wiser heart, one that was willing to drink in everything. But all I could do was stand in front of the picture and weep. I used to be so angry, I thought—and I didn't even know why half the time. I missed so much, let so many days roll by, not realizing how fast they were going, and now they've come back to ache inside me.

In the midst of my tears, I decided what to get my father for Christmas: a book of photographs of horses. So he can remember how good they are for the inside of him, so that in his dreams he can mount his horse and take jumps like he used to, so time can turn around and take him along, return him to more carefree days.

THE ASSASSINATION OF Yitzhak Rabin brought the world up short; for the past few days, I could feel grief on the streets, as well as shock. I thought of how my father could have come up with soothing words, the way he did after the *Challenger* disaster. There is a silent space where his voice would be. The White House asked my mother to go to Israel for Rabin's service, to represent my father; she felt she couldn't and asked George Shultz to go instead. I know it was not only that she felt uncomfortable leaving my father on such short notice; it was also that attending a funeral such as Rabin's would have been too painful a task. In some ways, the pain would have been a link between the past and a future that's hovering up ahead. Rabin was shot just after he gave a speech—the same way my father was shot. And the solemn gathering of world leaders is something that my family will eventually experience in the most personal of ways. I don't think my mother could have endured looking into the shadows of what lies ahead—having the world watch her mourn a fallen leader, when soon enough the world will be watching her mourn her husband.

I cut out from the newspaper the speech Rabin's granddaughter gave at his funeral; her eloquence, the poetry of her words, broke my heart and made me stand in awe of a seventeen-year-old girl who could shape grief into such beautiful thoughts.

She said, "You were the pillar of fire in front of the camp and now we are left in the camp alone, in the dark;

and we are so cold and so sad." She closed by saying, "I imagine angels are accompanying you now, and I ask them to take care of you because you deserve their protection."

I have the clipping tucked under some papers at my desk so I can look at it often—for inspiration, for a feeling of connection to someone who has gone through the difficulty of mourning in the glare of the world's spotlight, and because I can learn from this young girl.

# NOVEMBER 1995, LOS ANGELES

Somewhere over the middle of the country, at thirty thousand feet, I began crawling into myself, becoming so comfortable with silence that talking seemed to require great effort. Maybe part of it had to do with not seeing my father for a couple of months and knowing things had gotten worse. I closed my eyes on the plane so that stewardesses wouldn't ask me questions I would have to answer. It was a state of calm, of distance, that I couldn't shake, and I wasn't really sure I wanted to.

"Are you okay?" my mother asked that evening after I had dinner with my parents and she was showing me some photographs in the bedroom.

"Yes, I'm just tired from the flight and the time difference," I told her, struggling to move myself forward, outward, to be more present, less reserved. But I was having trouble pulling myself out of my own shadows, and I wasn't sure I could explain why.

It came to me late that night, lying in bed in my hotel room, listening to the crash of the surf outside. My father's quietness is what fascinates me now; he looks out from a place I can't get to, can only wonder about. All I can do is hope that if I grow quiet enough myself, some intuitive knowledge might take over and help me understand. I might meet him somewhere within that silence and suddenly be able to decipher the map of thoughts behind it.

Years ago—so long ago now it seems like another life—I would wait beside my father in the ocean for the next set of waves. We didn't talk very much. I remember the pull of tides around my legs, the wide, empty horizon, and the rhythm of his breathing. I matched my breathing to his, knowing even then that I needed to memorize those easy blue hours—the afternoons when we had nothing else to do but wait for the next set of waves.

Now, on Thanksgiving morning, my father waited for me on the bike path outside the beach hotel where I stay. He was with the man who assists him and a few Secret Service agents. I wanted to take him down closer to the water, but he wasn't sure if he wanted to cross the sand—I'm not sure why. It was a warm day, but he was in a long-sleeved shirt with a sweater over it. My father used to spend summer days on the beach in a bathing suit; he always smelled like Coppertone.

As we stood on the bike path, I was aware of people noticing him and smiling, but hanging back, reluctant to intrude. Even the one man who asked me politely if he could say hello to my father did so gently, deferentially. He shook my father's hand, said, "I just wanted to say hello to you," and then moved on. He didn't try to start up a conversation of any kind, and I felt he was showing respect for the disease my father has admitted to having—one which makes conversation difficult.

Eventually, we walked down to the water's edge to watch the surfers. The waves were up, and only accomplished surfers were out on the water. Spotting a yellow lifeguard truck, I said, "Look, Dad—they didn't have fancy jeeps like that when you were a lifeguard, did they?"

He shook his head no and kept watching the waves and the surfers. "I lifeguarded for a lot of summers," he said.

"At the river, right?" I asked.

"Yes . . . but the river had its ways."

That comment kept echoing through my mind. The river had its ways. I knew what he meant—the deceptively smooth surface fooled naive swimmers who didn't know about the deep currents. But his words took me back to all that he had taught me about nature—about the power beneath its often-calm appearance, the power that must be respected, revered. I've heard his lifeguard stories. He knew where the currents were treacherous; he learned about them and became a strong enough swimmer to save others who were weaker and less knowledgeable about the ways of the river. Always his stories and his instructions to me about the sea or the land or animals seemed to provide me with life lessons as well. I was told to always get back on a horse after falling off so that fear wouldn't have a chance to set in.

"What if I break my leg or my arm or something?" I remember asking once.

"Well, that would be an exception to the rule," he conceded as he helped me back onto the horse I had just fallen off.

It's echoed throughout my life: Get back on after you fall off, so fear won't set in.

I also heard, laced into his comment about the river, his acceptance of life—the pull of its tides and currents, its unexpected dangers.

The river has its ways . . . so does the sea, so does life. He's letting its currents take him; he's not fighting them. They're pulling him out now, and he's going willingly— on his way to heaven—as unafraid as he was so many years ago when he would turn his back on a huge wave, start swimming to catch it, and yell "Swim!" to me so I wouldn't miss the ride.

Why couldn't we stay like that forever? some small voice in me keeps asking. I have never matched my father's fearlessness. The march of time scares me—the currents beneath the surface that I can't control and can't swim against.

On this bright Thanksgiving morning, we turned away from the sea and walked back across the sand. Somewhere behind us, in the vast miles of blue ocean, a young girl, trying to be fearless, was swimming furiously to catch a wave and ride it to shore beside her father.

He walks more slowly now. I held his arm, matched my steps to his. Our feet kicked up puffs of white sand. We're both older now, and only one of us remembers clearly all the sun-drenched days long ago when we swam together in the ocean and rode waves. But some things don't change—I'm still trying to be as fearless as my father is.

WHEN I WAS YOUNGER, Thanksgiving seemed to start days before the actual date. Preparations for the meal, setting the table, planning for relatives—like my grandparents and my aunt and uncle, whom we didn't see that often—gave the holiday a busyness, an edge of excitement that I liked as a child and was disdainful of as a teenager who had learned to be disdainful of everything. This Thanksgiving was quiet and made me sad. My grandparents are gone, my uncle is not well—he and my aunt don't come to Los Angeles anymore—and there were no Thanksgiving smells wafting through the house for long hours before the meal. My mother had ordered the dinner from the country club where my father plays golf; she went down to pick it up in the afternoon. We were a small family, trying too hard to make this a festive occasion, when the truth was that we were all fighting against the sadness that grows even deeper with holidays. We ate early because my father tires easily now, and I drove back to the beach chased by memories, ensnared by this waiting game we're all part of.

My mother and I flew back to New York early Saturday morning. As we were saying goodbye to my father, telling him that we were leaving together, he repeated, "You're flying to New York together?"

"Yes," my mother told him.

His eyes were sparkling when he said, "That's what I like to see."

At night now, before I go to sleep, I talk to my father. I tell him we will be all right, and he'll still be able to watch us, look down on us, and smile at the relationship he always wanted us to have. I don't know if my thoughts reach him, if my words travel thousands of miles and filter into his dreams. But I was taught to believe in such things. He always told me that God carries messages, catches dreams and wishes and transports them, so I imagine him listening, understanding, and smiling.

## DECEMBER 1995

I've taken up ice-skating—suddenly, passionately—like falling in love. One day it was the farthest thing from my mind; the next I couldn't think of anything else. I went skating one afternoon with two friends at Wollman Rink in Central Park, and discovered that my body had no recollection of ever having skated as a child, although I did go to a skating rink occasionally in California. Decades later, I couldn't find my center of balance, couldn't stop being afraid, and couldn't let go of my friend's arm. As foolish as I looked and felt, I knew I was hooked. I bought skates, scheduled lessons, and tried to explain to puzzled friends that I couldn't stand not being good at something.

But it was more than that. Over the last couple of weeks, as I've found my balance and inched past my fear, I've come to understand this new passion. Part of it has to do with the sheer beauty of the sport, and the solitude, the quiet isolation of gliding across the ice. I walk across the park just after dawn, bundled up against the cold, with my ice skates in my gym bag. Only a few other skaters are out at that hour; they're graceful, impressive, but tolerant of the novice whose efforts they understand. I suppose some of them know who I am, but it doesn't matter—in that early, cold hour of the morning, I'm someone learning to skate, and they give me tips, encouragement. Mostly, they leave me alone to find the balance they know will come.

Twice a week, I take lessons, but on other days I go around the rink on my own, listening to the scrape of my blades on the ice, to the quiet of the park at that hour, and to the classical music that's usually playing. It's an escape I crave. I get up before dawn, have my coffee as the sun is coming up, and then head across the park like a kid going to her favorite activity. Now I just tell friends that it makes me happy.

There is something about skating that is beyond the sport itself; the balance, the grace, and the fluidity are the way I would like to go through life. I think often now of what my father taught me about life when he taught me to ride a horse and to bodysurf.

"The horse always knows if you're afraid," he would tell me. "You can never hide that; he just feels it. You have to remember that he has no idea he's bigger than you. He's waiting for you to tell him what you want. But if he feels that you're afraid, then he'll get frightened and confused."

About swimming in the ocean, riding the waves, he said, "If you don't turn your back on the wave and trust in your own strength as a swimmer, you'll miss the ride. You'll fall off the back of the wave or else get pounded by it."

My skating instructor pointed out to me that my balance gets shaky only when I get scared. It was as if the echo of my father's voice were poised on the wind, coming back to me through someone else.

THE BIGGEST SNOWSTORM we've had so far
this winter began late in the night. I could almost feel, in
my sleep, the snowfall beginning, blanketing the city. I
woke up from a dream that keeps revisiting me, in different forms and scenes, but with one central figure: Sadie,
the dog who was my faithful companion for ten years until
the summer before last, when she died in my arms. She's
come into my dreams three times this week. At the
moment of her death, she taught me how it feels when a
soul flutters away—my arms will never forget it. She
taught me to say goodbye, and in the weeks that followed,
she taught me how to grieve.

I've come to think of her as a sweet spirit willing to
visit me when I need her the most, winging back from
eternity's shadows to remind me that death isn't an
ending; it's just another place. A few months after Sadie
died, I was awakened sometime after midnight with the
clear sensation that she had jumped onto the end of my
bed, as she was wont to do often during our long relationship, knowing she wasn't supposed to but thinking I
might not wake up and notice her. I sat up, certain that I
would see her curled up at the foot of the bed, startled
when I didn't. My tears came in a flood just as they did in
the weeks following her death—a gentle counsel about the
nature of grief. It has no beginning or ending, no boundaries. It ebbs and flows, and changes us forever.

For three nights running, Sadie has come back to me
in the crowded hallways of that mysterious realm we call
dreams. She's returned healthy and young, without the
pain and infirmities that marked the end of her life. In one

dream, she was keeping my mother company, staying close to her, licking her face and nuzzling her the way dogs do when they know a human is hurting. In another, we were back at my childhood home in California. The details of the dream blurred as soon as I woke up, but Sadie's presence was clear, unmistakable.

It seemed fitting, after leaving her again in dreamtime, that I would wake up this morning to a transformed world—white, shivering, with snowflakes angling past my windows. When I was a child, I used to complain that it didn't snow in Los Angeles, and it wasn't right because Christmas is supposed to have snow. My father would bundle me up in stories about snowstorms and cold, driving winds; he brought winter to me in my imagination, transforming the world—for a while at least.

By afternoon, the storm had turned fierce. It was a relentless storm front, exciting in spite of its inconveniences. This brutal side of nature makes me think of Vikings and hearty sailors forging ahead in the face of nature's fury.

We do push on—especially New Yorkers, who probably were Vikings in past lives. When the city is under siege by a winter storm, people stubbornly carry on—either unkindly or generously, studies in the best and worst of human nature. Strangers help elderly people across slippery intersections while others ignore them. A blind man on Columbus Avenue was calling out, "Can someone please help me to the subway?" I heard him from a block away. The snow was blowing hard, and people were rushing past him. I knew I was going to be the one to help him across Columbus to the steps leading down to the subway, and I noticed, as he took my arm, passers-by averting their eyes, looking down or away as if they hadn't seen him, hadn't heard him calling out. They had Christmas shopping to do, errands; they were in a hurry to get out of the cold, get home. When I left him, I thought, I'll forget about him, too. I'll return to the pressures and the clutter of the holidays, and the man will be on some other street corner calling out for someone to help him.

THE STORM HAS BEEN getting worse by the hour, threatening to cripple the city. But it can't, really, because life has to go on. It's a magnified version of the thought I carry with me each day. My father is drifting farther and farther away; one day soon he'll let go. Yet the world will go on. It will pause, mourn, but the ordinariness of life will continue.

A girlfriend of mine in Los Angeles just lost her mother, who had been suffering from Alzheimer's for many years. She died in my friend's living room, with family around her, after hanging on for several days. She finally let go when my friend told her it was all right, that she could leave, that there was no reason to stay here anymore and be sick. While the story was being told to me on the phone, my friend's daughter needed help with her homework, her youngest child was clamoring to be fed . . . I heard the sounds of life going on as usual, because it has to.

Another friend's mother had a stroke recently. Christmas will be spent taking care of her because the nurse they hired quit just after Thanksgiving. Her mother has limited movement on one side and can't speak. But she can sing—a different part of the brain controls singing.

For all of us, life's responsibilities and mundane duties still have to be attended to. We do our work, buy Christmas presents, try not to catch a cold in the flu-infested winter months; we worry about running up our credit cards. We grieve, cry, and still go on.

Life goes on, but it goes on differently. We're quieter, more reflective. When friends call, they often ask if they've woken us up because our voices sound dreamy, distant. It is sort of like waking up—the phone rings, and we return to the world, carrying on but with a part of us still far away. We pause even in the middle of Manhattan and look up at a brilliant sunset or a full moon. We take time with things like that, absorb them on a deeper level, because we've learned how short this life is and how much beauty can be missed along the way. We became students of life's brevity by watching a loved one's time grow short. It doesn't matter what the disease is or the cause; we struggle through the same web of feelings. We get tangled, snagged, pulled under by emotions that seem overwhelming.

Perhaps dreams are one way we're helped through. The subconscious moves in with its intricate magic, soothes us at night. Lately, my mother's dreams have been of earlier years with my father—times that must have felt like forever to her then. She's told me that the dreams are vivid, so real they feel more like time travel. They are a tonic to her, a way to come in from the cold of a future that's bearing down like winter. My dreams about Sadie are doing the same for me—reminding me that I survived the abyss of pain that opened up inside me when she died. And that I not only survived it, I changed—became more relaxed, a bit softer, less frightened of life's surprises.

My father was with Sadie a few times during the ten years that she was mine—not often, I suppose, but understandable given the long stretches of time when I was resolutely estranged from my parents. I noticed how she would leave my side and wander over to my father, curl up at his feet or—more accurately—on them. The first time, she glanced back at me as if to say, I'm sorry. I love you, but I need to lie on his feet, stay close to him.

In a way, she's doing the same thing now—in spirit form, as a messenger from the other side. By coming into my dreams, she's letting me know that she'll be there helping him across—an innocent soul who has traveled the dark waters between this world and the next and carries with her the knowledge that it's a more peaceful place, a place where weary travelers are restored, renewed.


MY MOTHER USED TO SAY, whenever someone was hurt or ill or died over the Christmas holidays, "It seems so much sadder when these things happen around Christmastime."

Now we're going through our own sad Christmas. She is decorating the house, but it's a lonely, obligatory ritual. My mind has been spinning back to memories of childhood Christmases when the choreography of the season was so set, so dependable.

Just after Thanksgiving, my father would put up

Christmas lights on the outside of the house. I would follow him around, holding up strings of lights and feeding them to him up on his ladder. It took most of the afternoon, but by dinnertime, colored lights edged our roof, heralding a season that, as children, we looked forward to all year. We used to have a tree delivered—flocked, which I think is illegal now because of fire concerns, but no one thought of that then, and no one I know went up in flames. Then we had tree-decorating night. Whatever family squabbles were going on melted on that night. Some of the boxes or ornaments contained memories, ornaments my brother and I made in kindergarten. They were primitive, clumsy pieces of childhood art—bits of foil stuck to colored paper. Miraculously, some of them still survive. In the years before our family dwindled, my grandparents would fly in from Arizona and stay for a few days; my aunt and uncle would spend Christmas Day with us. A steady stream of friends would arrive, visit, drink eggnog and sherry. There was chaos, excitement, warmth, love, and a sweet exhaustion at nightfall.

Now my mother and I acknowledge that we both fear this will be my father's last Christmas. We mention it cautiously, hesitantly, easing ourselves into the subject. People learn to talk about death in stages, and we are no exception. You start out shy, uncomfortable, and get bolder as time goes on. The emotions that bubble to the surface evoke other feelings—guilt, for example. When you first realize that you're starting to see death as a release, a beginning rather than an ending, when you look into the future and know that, along with sorrow, there will be relief, the guilt almost chokes you. It takes time to share those feelings with someone else; you think they're yours alone, and there must be something wrong with you, something cold at your core.

I began introducing to my mother the idea that this time, right now, may be the hardest, that after my father dies there will be a different kind of pain, but the waiting will be over, the anxiety of wondering how bad things will get. We all want my father to leave this world with dignity. The only way to do that with a disease like Alzheimer's is if death beats it to the finish line. So you start to rethink the mythology about death, the old paradigms that you've held on to—the Grim Reaper, a dark, shrouded angel. I have an image now that when my mother and I talk about death, we are approaching a beautiful woman; yet we're still not sure we're supposed to find her beautiful, so we speak softly, tentatively. We touch the hem of her garment and feel better, more at peace. Some deeper knowledge starts to take shape; wouldn't a loving God send a beautiful, kind angel to take someone away, knowing all the fear that is attached to dying?

AS I PACKED my suitcase for the holidays, I started to wonder if I should pack more black clothes, just in case. My father was always taking life as it came; I was always searching for crystal balls and fortune-tellers. In the end, I struck a balance—I put in one black suit. I considered packing my ice skates and looking for an indoor rink somewhere in Los Angeles, even though I knew it was impractical. But I was reluctant to take even a temporary break from skating. As I stood looking at my bulging suitcase, lamenting that there was no room for my skates, I got an image of my father's eyes watching me with amusement. I could almost hear him, saying something like, You can still keep the feeling with you even when you're not actually skating.

I left my skates behind, left the snow and the winter weather to fly into California's seventy-degree climate, which I still find so inappropriate for Christmas.

## CHRISTMAS HOLIDAYS 1995, LOS ANGELES

I peeled off my winter clothes and put on shorts and a T-shirt. Before going up to my parents' house, I took a long walk on the beach and lingered on the sand while a brilliant sunset cascaded across the sky. The child of a patient man who believed in pausing for sunsets, I couldn't tear myself away; I sat on the beach until the red melted into purple. Help me make my father's passage easy, I asked God, as the sun made its dramatic descent.

Buddhists believe there is a body of dark water between this world and the next which a soul must travel across. They light lanterns to help the soul make its journey safely. Show me how to light lanterns for my father, I prayed, so he can leave with a willing heart and calm thoughts.

When I walked into my parents' house, my father greeted me as if he'd just seen me the other day. Time does strange things for someone with Alzheimer's; it becomes compressed around some events, speeds past others. Occasionally, chunks of time simply vanish. More and more, when I'm around my father, I try to forget my own awareness of time and pick up on his. My mother was busy with last-minute Christmas decorations; he and I were alone in

the den. There is an awkwardness now in starting a conversation; it's never a certainty that he'll become engaged
in whatever subject I bring up.

"I've taken up ice-skating, Dad," I told him.

"Oh," he said, his face brightening. "How's that
going?"

"Great. I'm not very good yet—I just started—but I
really love it."

"I used to ice-skate," he began, and I heard his voice
settle, become more certain, comfortable in the terrain
of a memory that was still vivid. "Every winter when I
was a kid. In Dixon, Illinois, on the Rock River. It was
about two blocks wide and ran through the center of
town. That's what we did in the winter—skated on the
river."

"Were you good?" I already knew the answer. My
father was a natural athlete, easy and confident.

"Yes," he said. "I was a very good skater."

"I wish you could have taught me."

A puzzled look passed across his eyes before he asked,
"Didn't we ever do that?"

"No," I told him. "Ice-skating isn't a real big priority
in California. But you taught me other things. Like how
to ride a horse and get back on after I fell off. You taught
me to bodysurf big waves and not be afraid."

He shook his head casually, knowingly. "There's
nothing to be afraid of with the ocean," he said.

"Have you ever been afraid of anything?"

"Oh, sometimes, a little, you know." He pointed to
his solar plexus, vaguely, waving his hand across as if fear
were a feeling that blew through at moments but never set
down roots.

"It's like a flutter inside, but then it disappears?"
I asked.

"Yes. It's like that—it just passes."

"Well, I'm trying. I'm still trying to not be afraid," I
assured him. Tears were escaping from my eyes.

"The river was wonderful," he said, still caught in his
memory. "You could watch everything move across it."

"Like the seasons?"

He nodded. "We swam there in the summers and
skated in the winters."

A river ran through his town. It always comes back to
the river, I thought, with all its symbolism, all its
metaphors. He's content to return there; in a sense, he's
never left. It's constant; it has its mysteries, its currents; it
transforms with the seasons, marking time in the most
poetic of ways, with colors, textures, moods—raging in
gray anger during storms, lapping peacefully through
summer's long, blue days, becoming an icy playground
in winter. The river was how my father learned about life.
In the end it will be there, carrying him away.

I knew this was why I'd taken up skating, as I sat in
my parents' home, missing it already. In a strange, long-
distance way, it's bringing me closer to my father, to who
he used to be. He can't teach me now, but something
whispers to me when I put on my skates and go out to the
ice. He thought we must have done that together, he must
have passed that on to me. You're teaching me now, I
wanted to say to him, but didn't because I was afraid such
a comment might confuse him.

I mentioned skating to him again on Christmas
morning as we walked along the beach; Rollerbladers sped
past us on the bike path.

"I bet you were a really fast skater, weren't you?" I asked him.

"Yep," he said without hesitating. "I was a good skater. I was very fast."

At that moment, I knew I would someday be able to say that about myself.

The world looks strange to my father now—increasingly unfamiliar. I could see it in his eyes when he looked at passersby; I heard it in his self-conscious, gentle laugh—head tilted slightly, his shoulders shrugging in that bemused way that's always been part of his charm, that "there you go again" shrug. But then his eyes lifted to watch seagulls in flight, and I saw them relax; taking wing seemed to be something he could comprehend. I watched him as he watched the gulls and wondered if at that moment his spirit was longing for flight.

MY BROTHER MICHAEL, his family, and Maureen, her husband, and child were there for Christmas Day, all of us trying to pretend we weren't as sad as we were. Ron needed to stay in Seattle, and there was a moment when I thought my father was going to ask where he was. He didn't, but I still think that it occurred to him.

Families are inherently unmanageable—ragtag armies at times, yet with a unity even they don't fully understand. Someone is always pulling a thread, throwing the whole thing askew. Yet the threads remain, binding us to one another even when geography and other priorities pull us apart. Christmas seems to magnify everything; the season is never smooth, is always dramatic in one way or another. My father probably had the clearest viewpoint of all—Ron may have been in Seattle, but he wasn't as far away as it seemed.

My Christmas gift to my father was a photography book, *Horses of the Sun,* by Robert Vavra. The pictures of horses are so real, so vivid, their eyes gaze out of the pages with such calm dignity, anyone who has known horses and loved them can't help but be transfixed by the images. My father retreated into the book as I had hoped he would. I could only wonder about the memories that were stirred up; his face had the same serene look that it used to have when we rode together at the ranch, when he was doing what he loved so much—riding his horse along trails and hillsides, exulting in that magical communion between human and animal.

EVER SINCE LAST SPRING, when I went out to our old ranch after twenty-five years, I've been dreaming about it, longing to go back again. My one visit in the spring was to film a Father's Day tribute for *E! Entertainment;* there were other people with me, I was working, so I couldn't really get lost in the experience of returning to one of the most cherished places of my childhood, and I desperately wanted to.

The day after Christmas, I drove out just after dawn. Once into the familiar cradle of mountains, I remembered how the morning chill lasted longer, how the sun was slower to warm the earth. So much still looked the same— the ranch is part of the park system, so it's remained undeveloped, but the fences are gone; some of the neighboring ranches have changed in appearance.

California has had little rain this year; the fields were

the color of wet ash. The duck pond was dry—not even a small pool of water remained to indicate that it's supposed to be a pond. I know there were drought years when I was growing up. I must have seen it like this before, yet my memories are of a lush, verdant landscape or its summer version—golden and sunbaked. As I walked down the main trail that cuts through the center of the property, my memories stood stubbornly alongside the land I was surrounded by; I wasn't sure which was more real.

I needed to return to this ranch, to touch again the life we once had here. There were long, slow days when the rest of the world seemed far away, inconsequential. That was before the world came to own my father in the particular way a life in politics has of claiming people, redefining them. When I was younger, days at the ranch were filled by riding, swimming, hiking. My father cleared brush, made new trails, built jumps from telephone poles. My mother picked armsful of lilacs that bloomed by the fence around our tiny ranch house. I don't remember the sound of a ringing telephone, although I know there was one in the barn, used mainly to call the vet or the blacksmith for the horses' shoes. In those days, my father was my teacher; I learned to jump a horse, ride a proper English saddle. Things would never be that simple again; the world would never be that far away.

We planted young pine trees around the ranch house. Now they are towering, the house is gone, and I couldn't find the lilac bushes. It was difficult to get my bearings in that part of the property. But the rest of it—the open land—is a map of my youth. Ghosts of cattle lingered beneath the tree they always favored, around that one bend in the trail. I found the path to the top of my favorite hill—the one we used to gallop up. I walked up it this morning, so many years later, yet I could still hear the sound of horses' hooves, still see my father ahead of me, leaning forward to give his horse more rein.

After he became governor of California, there were days on horseback—on different ranches, one in Sacramento, which I never particularly liked, and later on the ranch in Santa Barbara, which has a special magic. But the days were never the same because he was on loan then, owned by the job he had chosen to do, had been elected to do. The world couldn't be left behind anymore. I wanted to return to the land that held my first memories—of the days that went by so fast.

ON MY LAST NIGHT in Los Angeles, as I was leaving my parents' house, I knelt down beside my father's chair and told him I wouldn't be seeing him the next day; I was going home to New York in the morning. When I saw his eyes locked on mine, I said, "Dad, I want you to know that whatever happens to you, we'll be all right. I'll take care of Mom—she'll be all right."

Earlier in the day, my mother and I had agreed that he might need to hear one of us tell him this—so he could feel calm about leaving. I knew it would be difficult for my mother, so I did it.

"Okay," he said, but his eyes said more. They told me he understood, that he grasped everything I was trying to express.

I got on the plane the next morning wondering if I would see him again. He used to tell a story about the last time he saw his own father. Moved by some kind of premonition, he hugged him goodbye rather than shaking his hand, as he usually did. His premonition was right—his father died shortly after without their seeing each other again.

In my father's pocket, he keeps what he calls his lucky coins. One of them says "Let go and let God." I left Los Angeles holding on to the image of that coin, mentally putting it into my own pocket—a reminder of how to handle life's hairpin turns.

As the plane took me home—back to winter, to the faster pace of New York—I looked down at the land I was flying over, at the clusters of cities, long expanses of desert, red-rock canyons, and distant snow-covered peaks. I wondered when my father fell in love with this country. Was he flying over it when it struck him—an overwhelming surge of emotion that would change his life forever?

Most of us have a less-intense relationship with the country we call our homeland. Our feelings are seasonal, fickle at times, varied. We have times of anger, of indifference, moments when we are annoyed by what our country represents; our loyalty is constant, but not always passionate. My father was in love with America; the national anthem could move him to tears and sometimes did. It was something I gradually became aware of, yet I still don't fully understand.

I came of age being angry at America—I and many others—for sending our peers, our classmates, off to Vietnam. One boy I went to school with joined the marines and returned with his body intact but with his spirit damaged. I still have his letters; they document the slaughter of his soul.

I was angry at America years later for appropriating my father, first as governor, then as president. How could I encroach on my father's time when an entire country, and at times the world, demanded his attention? At least that was my perception at the time. Sorry, he belongs to me, I imagined America saying—you'll just have to step aside. I remember having a fleeting thought, when my father was elected president, that no one could stop me from moving to Switzerland and changing my citizenship. I wasn't angry at my father; I was furious at America.

Now the country I have felt such anger toward is nestled beside my family, quietly waiting for the moment we all know will come—when my father takes his last breath. He brought America into this private, painful journey as if she were another member of our family. He composed a handwritten letter to her, sharing his private thoughts and wishes for the future, bowing away gracefully, asking for nothing. Now I gain sustenance from the country's knowledge of the passage we're going through. If we didn't have that companionship, the loneliness would be unbearable. America no longer seems a formidable opponent; she's just there, enveloping us, sharing our grief, waiting.

Something curious happened to me on my first morning back in New York. I walked across the park to the skating rink, and when I got out on the ice, I discovered I wasn't afraid anymore. My balance was better, my movements cleaner, smoother, and I felt in my body the transformational beauty of the sport—the thing that sends people out on cold mornings to skate until their toes go numb. For an hour, I was transported. I was on a river in a small town where kids pull their ice skates out from under their beds as soon as the temperature turns freezing and spend long hours skating on the river. For that brief time, the real world fell away from me. I wasn't in Manhattan; it wasn't 1996; the days were sweeter, and the world was younger.

# JANUARY 1996

My father has been feeling ill, off and on, for the past two days. The doctor has come, but this is beyond the boundaries of medicine, and we all know it. His body is responding to his spirit's wish to leave. But he's torn; we know that, too. Even his doctor told my mother that my father might be staying here for her. I've suggested to her that some of the weightiness she feels is that responsibility. If he's hanging on for her, then she has the difficult task of instructing her heart to let him go.

I had considered that he might die over the holidays while I was home—my instinct was that the time was that close. But obviously it wasn't meant to happen that way. Now I've thought that perhaps I'm not supposed to be there. Maybe my father's passing should be experienced only by him and my mother, a private sojourn for two people who entwined their lives, their hearts, and who need to be alone to part ways.

People are, finally and uniquely, who they have always been to us. Our parents are ultimately that—nothing else. Throughout our lives, we may have given them other roles to play—friends, enemies, even rivals. But when the final moment comes—the cleaving that is like nothing we've known before—we say goodbye only to our parents. It's their hands we let go of, their hands we still find ourselves reaching for until the permanence of their passing redefines us. We come full circle; at death, our parents are purely, and forever, who they were at our birth.

My mother is losing her soulmate. The parting has a language and a depth all its own; it's intricate, mysterious, dismantles the heart and remolds it like nothing else in life.

"You've had nothing to prepare you for this," I said to my mother in a recent conversation about the tidal waves of emotion that wash over her. "You've never been through this before."

"Yes, I have," she countered. "With my father and then with my mother."

"It's not the same thing," I reminded her.

IT'S SUCH A STRANGE sensation to know that someone's time is near. There is a calm to it, a serenity; you give in completely to the act of waiting, linger along the fringes of your daily life, yet with a lucidity, a clarity, that seems to have come on suddenly, miraculously. It's not just me—I've heard others speak of this as well.

I imagine the phone ringing in the middle of the night, or just before dawn, and I wonder if I'll wake up suddenly just before it rings. Will some flash of intuition jolt me out of sleep? I've had nights in which I've woken up abruptly with my thoughts racing across the continent to my parents. I've lain awake waiting for the phone to ring—the call I fear will come one of these days or nights.

Yesterday, I accidentally knocked from a table a tiny glass frog that my father gave me many years ago. Frogs are considered lucky in some religion or culture, although I can't remember which one. Maybe right now, I thought, as I picked up the tiny figure, grateful that it hadn't broken. I could imagine it that way—a gift from my father falling to the floor at the precise moment his soul flew upward.

When I was ice-skating this morning, there was a moment when everything seemed hushed, poised silently on the edge of some mystery as if the entire world were holding its breath. It's usually quiet, with skaters lost in their own thoughts, their own work, talking quietly if they talk at all. But this was different—beyond the usual quiet. It turned out to be just a lull—uneventful. Or maybe it was only my imagination.

I wonder about the color of the day; will it be silvery and cold when it happens, or will there be sunlight? Will the sky suddenly change? Will clouds scud across it, or pull apart as if to welcome his spirit?

In January 1981, when my father was sworn in as president, the day was gray and overcast until he stood up to speak, and then a shaft of sunlight sliced the clouds apart and shone on him like a spotlight. After he had finished, the sky closed up again, returning the day to the same somber color it had been before. When my father was shot, Mike Deaver stayed awake all night—that long, horrible night when rain fell relentlessly. At dawn, there was a rainbow over the White House. Mike got to his camera in time to capture it; my mother still has the photograph. At dramatic moments of my father's life, the sky has seemed to respond in kind, changing in some way, so I wonder about the moment when he moves on. I keep a watchful eye on the heavens these days.

Lately, the weather has been moody, as if it can't make up its mind. It's been icy, freezing, but today the temperature has steadily risen. People are walking around without gloves or hats. The snow is melting, causing flooding; there are small rivers at the intersections. At midday, a rainstorm blew in on fierce winds that howled outside my windows. I stayed home and wrote, dressed in sweatpants and one of my father's shirts. Over the holidays I asked my mother for one—spurred perhaps by the memory of her sleeping with a shirt of his the night he was shot and lay in the hospital with tubes and drains, under the steady watch of alert nurses. She gave me two white shirts, finely made, monogrammed. "RWR" is stitched on the left side just below my heart, in gray thread. It's the same color as the day outside. Everything seems significant right now—an omen, a promise, a gentle turning of the wheel. You can go, I keep telling my father in my prayers. This struggle is too difficult—it tears at the spirit. It's a soft haunting that stirs us awake at night, leaves us staring into the darkness, listening to nothing, waiting for something.

I fill up my sleepless hours with prayers. I send some directly to my father, certain that in those still, suspended hours before sleep closes in, the channels are open and he'll hear me. Metaphysicians and some psychologists believe the mind is at its most powerful just before sleep; the thought waves are pure, unencumbered. I imagine my prayers arching across the country, through time zones and storm tracks, to find my father in the space before dreams. Think of the seagulls, I tell him; think of their flight, their white shapes in the blue sky. Think of the quote you used to soothe a nation after the *Challenger* disaster—lines from the poem "High Flight": they "slipped the surly bonds of earth" to touch the face of God.

That's what I think you're doing when you look up at the sky and your eyes get soft, dreamy. You're seeing God's face—infused with light and patience, and more beauty than can ever be found on this earth. And then we pull you back, remind you that the "surly bonds of earth" are still holding you. Sometimes it's just with a question, some banal query like, What do you want for lunch? or Would you like to go for a walk? It doesn't matter—we've interrupted your communion, reeled you back; your eyes change, and the world grumbles on.

This world is surly—what a perfect word the poet chose. It struggles along, mired in its unhappiness, addicted to its darkest wishes, and it's getting worse. You used to tell me it would. You used to tell me about Jesus' return—you said it would happen in the world's darkest hour. It wasn't a frightening story—you didn't tell it that way. You made it mythological, adventurous. A world gone wrong—so foolish it couldn't find its way out of the shadows; so mean it didn't want to try. And then one man—Jesus—would return, and the earth and everyone on it would be transformed. I used to love that story; I would ask you for it often, sometimes at bedtime because I wanted to dream about it. Once I asked you for it on a day when I had pretended to be sick because David Lewis kept bullying me at school, and I couldn't stand it anymore. You knew I wasn't really sick, and you sat on my bed and talked to me about ignoring bullies, walking right past them as if they were air. I asked you for the story about the Second Coming then; I wanted to hear again about a world without meanness (without David Lewis, who had taught me what meanness was). I went back to school the next day, confident that someday Jesus would return, and at that point even David Lewis would turn friendly. Until then, I didn't have to look at him. He never bothered me again.

I was keeping a secret from you, though—I also thought Jesus was going to return to be my boyfriend. I would ask you for the story, give my imagination free rein, indulge my fantasies secretly. Until finally, one day, I told you.

"I think he's going to come back to marry me," I said.

You didn't miss a beat. You said, "Well, he's going to be very busy. He's going to have a world to save."

But you didn't say no. I have always thought of that moment as one of great love. You allowed my heart room to daydream, to be young and unrealistic. You allowed me to gaze into the future and see whatever I wanted.

I want to return that love now, that one gesture, that sweet gift. I don't want to pull you back to this earth, to the bleakness of this world. I want to let you gaze upward and keep going. I know God's face is waiting and watching with such love, any of us would long to touch it. But we're not ready to see it yet, and you are.

I suppose that's what love finally comes to—a willingness to let someone go, into their dreams, their imaginations, or into another realm.

I'm going to remember your eyes looking upward. I'm going to remember the map they drew, the path they marked. This way—upward—past the bonds that hold us.

## February 1996, Los Angeles

I brought only one small suitcase with me—enough for two nights and one day. It was a trip designed for a good case of jet lag. As the plane landed, I wondered if I should even bother to set my watch back three hours, but in the end I did.

It was the day before my father's eighty-fifth birthday. At twilight, as I left the beach to go see my parents, the lines from an old Robbie Robertson song ran through my mind: "Don't leave me alone at twilight, twilight is the loneliest time of day." There is a solitariness, an isolation, to what my family is going through right now. The world is aware of our situation, yet we draw the curtains protectively around my father, preserving his dignity, his privacy, and our own. The world can know, but it doesn't get to see.

My mother told me that she's been having dreams about the ranch—not the one I grew up on, but the one they own now, north of Santa Barbara. She said, "I dream about the weekends we used to spend there—riding, sitting by the fireplace—the way it was before, when we were normal."

The hills of Bel-Air were shadowy and deep green; they seemed to fold around me as I turned off Sunset

Boulevard. I thought about the two nights ahead of me. My father's birthday would be celebrated twice—once privately, with family, on this twilit February evening, and publicly on Tuesday night.

My father was in the den when I came into my parents' house, sitting in his favorite chair, the most comfortable armchair in the den; it has deep cushions and faces the television. I don't remember his having a favorite chair when I was younger, and I sort of like it that he does now; it's quaint, fatherly, something out of a storybook. He stood up when I came into the room, like the gentleman his mother taught him to be. I no longer try to stop him; it's something ingrained in him. A woman enters the room, and he stands.

I found myself wishing that his birthday was being celebrated only on this one night, at home, quietly. I felt as if I were dragging with me the weight of my own confusion about the following night. Chasen's—the restaurant where my parents fell in love over countless dinners, the place where the elite of Hollywood could usually be seen, was being reopened for a lavish party for my father, who, of course, would be unable to attend. Chasen's closed its doors last year and was slated to be torn down for a shopping mall, but the surrounding neighborhood opposed the idea of another mall. It's remained intact, but boarded up—a ghost of the glittering restaurant it once was. Apparently Rupert Murdoch had something to do with convincing the owners to reopen it, allowing my father's birthday to be held there.

For weeks, I had been having trouble with this event, finding some balance point between a birthday celebration and the sadness that has become our constant companion in these waning days of my father's life. I didn't know what to do with a birthday celebration for someone who wouldn't be there because he wasn't well enough. I didn't feel celebratory; I felt off-balance, confused. Flying in and out of Los Angeles so quickly that I remained perpetually in the wrong time zone fit my jagged state of mind.

For a few nights before I went to California, I went up to the roof garden of my apartment building, bundled against the freezing temperatures, to plead with the stars for an answer. How do I handle this? I kept thinking. All I came up with was the word "bittersweet" as a way to put a label on the night. It's a word that doesn't give too much away, has a kind of dignity, a soft stoicism, hints at tears but conceals them. It was the best I could do.

My mother had lit candles on the table for our small birthday dinner. There were cards, a cake for dessert, and birthday wishes that he acknowledged politely but—I suspected—was somewhat indifferent to. Something had changed in him, in some deep, resolute part of his being. It was as if he had resolved a troubling question, settled on an answer, a decision. There was something lighter about him. I'll never know, but I thought that he had decided his time was near, and it had brought him peace of mind, a lightening of spirit.

While we were at the dinner table, Maureen pointed out the window to the moon rising above the city. A full moon—yellow, almost amber—was making its ascent in the clear night sky. We left the table and walked outside, as if pulled by it.

"The moon came up for your birthday, Dad," Maureen said.

I looked at my parents standing with their arms

around each other, my father winked at me, and I had a fleeting, sad thought—he will never see me in love the way I've seen him all these years. He'll never get to bask in my happiness as I have in his. It must seem strange to him, this solitary life I lead. I dated someone recently, briefly, but I ended it before the moon turned full. I knew it would never grow into the kind of love my parents have, and I'm spoiled now; I want nothing less.

While the moon rose in the sky, turned from amber to white, and we stood there spellbound, the life I have lived until now ached inside me. I wished I had outgrown my rebel ways earlier, fallen in love—deeply in love—had a child that my father could have held in his arms. Those things might still happen—love, motherhood—but he won't be here to see them.

TUESDAY WAS GRAY, foggy, at least by the beach where I spent most of the afternoon. My mother was busy with appointments, and my father went to play golf. I learned later that a helicopter hovered over the golf course with someone shooting pictures of him.

I had to be at Chasen's early to appear on *Larry King Live* with Maureen. The entire hour was being devoted to my father's birthday, with live and taped tributes from a wide spectrum of people. I appreciated what Larry King was doing, but I was still ensnared in my own conflicted feelings about having such a public event while we're going through a private trial.

I went by my parents' house first. I was flying out early the next morning, and I wanted to see my father again and visit with my mother before she and I had to walk into the media glare of the evening. The sound of male voices arguing met me when I walked into the house. My parents were in the den in front of the television set, which was turned to *Crossfire*. The participants were arguing about the "Reagan Revolution," "Reaganomics," the "Reagan legacy." I can't even say who the participants were because my attention became completely focused on my father. His name was being bandied about—harshly by one side, defensively by the other, but loudly, which seems to be a prerequisite for being on *Crossfire*. I studied his face, and he had an amused look in his eyes; I almost expected him to repeat his now-famous line from the Carter debate: "There you go again."

He's getting all of this, I thought. He's listening to this discussion about himself, and he's amused by it, the way he always was. He was always so comfortable in his own skin, in his own ideology, walking the terrain of his vision for America. You could dispute the ideology, disagree with the vision, but you were attracted to the man—to his modesty, his easiness about life. It was contagious; you found yourself calmed by his calm. He still has it, even now, listening to obstreperous men arguing in such an uncivilized manner, interrupting each other. He would never have done that; he never did. He'd watch the others with amusement. He had no use for vitriol or unpleasantness.

Tom Brokaw tells a story about grilling my father in an interview, asking him tough questions, not letting him off the hook, moving in for a journalist's kill. He was certain that even the unflappable Ronald Reagan must be crumbling under the pressure. But when they broke to change tape, my father stretched out his legs, looked at his

shoes, and said he had to find time later to get them
shined. Tom returned to the interview somewhat chastised
by the civility of the man he had been grilling.

WHEN *CROSSFIRE* WAS OVER, I had to get
to Chasen's. I said goodbye to my father, told him I loved
him, and he held my eyes longer than he usually does. "I
love you, too," he said. "Really." I wondered about it—the
added emphasis, the way he punctuated it with "really."
Part of me would remain with him all evening.

Chasen's felt like a restaurant that had only just
unsealed its doors. It felt unlived-in, like a house that had
been locked up for a long time. There was something stag-
nant about the air. I didn't want to pass all of the press,
lined up at the front entrance, so I was taken in through
the kitchen. Maureen was already there, and she noticed
something in my eyes. I have a tell-all face; I should never
take up poker.

"What's wrong?" she asked. "You can tell me—you
have a sister now to tell things to."

I told her my mixed feelings about the evening, and
her answer reflected the pragmatism she usually brings to
any challenge. We were being asked to speak for the
family, she told me, and we had to find whatever balance
we needed in order to do that. But what kept running
through my mind was what she had said first: "You have a
sister now. . . ." I lingered over that, shuffled through the
memories of our scattered history—more absences than
times together. We didn't grow up in the same household;
she lived with her mother, Jane Wyman, and visited
occasionally. We never raced each other to the breakfast

table, argued over who was going to feed the dog, invaded each other's rooms, borrowed things without asking. She was someone who came for Christmas, who moved east when I was a teenager and got married, then divorced. Her presence was felt more in letters and updates and photographs. When my long, dispiriting war with my mother stretched into decades, and into my adulthood, Maureen, like the rest of the family, retreated even further. It was self-preservation; the battlefield was too messy. Before Christmas of 1994, we had gone nine years without seeing each other.

She and I were hooked up with earpieces for *Larry King Live.* It was a satellite feed; he could see us, but we could only hear him in our ears, talk to him through clip-on microphones. Both Maureen and I had done this kind of thing countless times, but never together—never as sisters. We are getting to know each other now, after half our lives have been lived. Now, in this time of fighting shadows—the dark shape of our father's strange disease, the looming shadow of his death.

And we're different from each other, which sounds like an obvious statement, but it's something I never gave much thought to before. There are ways to draw boundary lines in interviews; people figure out what works for them only after being mercilessly invaded a number of times. There is a way to smile, a look in the eyes, a finality to sentences—it's subtle, but it usually works. During the interview, Maureen drew a boundary line between our public and private lives with cheerfulness; she gave the story a positive spin, but there was something about her smile that said, Stop right there. I allowed my mixed feelings to show in my eyes, believing that the thread of sadness also drew a line. We both did what we were asked to do, but in different ways, with our own expressions, our own syntax.

To Larry King's question about our father's health, Maureen said, "He's wonderful. The disease is horrible, but he's wonderful." End of sentence, end of answer, don't ask for more even though I'm smiling.

To his question of me: "What's your feeling about this evening?" I answered, "This is a bittersweet event. We're here to celebrate our father's birthday, but clearly he's not able to be here, so it's not entirely celebratory." I wasn't smiling; my eyes said, That's all you're getting, so don't push for more.

He didn't push either of us for more.

Through my earpiece I could hear others giving their comments and tributes to my father: both Ron and Michael, President Carter, Barry Goldwater, Lesley Stahl, Tom Brokaw . . . the list was impressive. And (I have to separate these men from the rest) Pat Buchanan and Bob Dole. I heard them praising my father in order to praise themselves—using him, clutching wildly to his coattails in their race for the presidency. According to each of them, they were carrying on Ronald Reagan's message, honoring his legacy. To me, they were co-opting his legacy for their own self-consumed goals at a time when he couldn't speak up for himself.

I was trying to keep my face immobile, clear of any visible feelings, because the camera could find me again at any moment. But I was thinking how ironic it was that I was not only feeling defensive about my father as a man, being used at a time like this, but I was also feeling defensive about his ideology—one I disagree with, but which was clearly being bastardized and misrepresented by at least two men so far this evening. I decided that, if he were well, he would still disagree with my politics, but he wouldn't agree with theirs either.

Then the third member of the Coattail Club walked in. I saw Newt Gingrich come into Chasen's and realized that he was going to sit in the booth with us for his part of *Larry King Live*. I whispered to Maureen, "Oh God, he's going to sit with us. God is really testing me tonight." A lesson in modern technology that I should have remembered: a clip-on microphone also picks up whispers. My comment was reported in a *Washington Post* gossip column two days later, and then in *Newsweek* and *New York* magazine.

But if God was testing me—which I do think he was, going on a friend's theory that God has a sense of humor—he might also have been out to teach me something. Because for the brief time that we sat in the same booth, Newt Gingrich seemed like a nice, easygoing person, and attuned to the fact that this was a difficult task for me—to be on camera commemorating my father's birthday while he was at home, not well enough to be there. I found myself putting politics aside for a few moments; here was a regular guy who probably enjoys kicking back with a beer. There was, however, a momentary suspension of that kindly feeling when he spoke into the camera and credited himself for carrying on the Reagan Revolution.

Indulging in the fantasy of what I wanted to say if I could, I thought, I don't remember my father ever suggesting that children should be taken away from mothers on welfare, as Mr. Gingrich did.

AFTER THE INTERVIEW, I had time to walk around Chasen's during the cocktail hour and observe an evening that was somewhat surreal. I overheard someone say that my mother had arrived, so I went looking for her. There were photographs placed around the restaurant— my parents in easier times, smiling, together, so much together that it baffled people. I imagined that she would avoid looking at those pictures for fear that they would usher in tears. I found her surrounded by a crush of people, all wanting to shake her hand, say something encouraging to her, have their moment with her. She made me think of an ambassador to a country that had changed, suffered a loss, but was still in need of an ambassador. Before, she would have shared the room with my father. Now she stood there alone, shaking hands, saying thank you, knowing some of the people well, some not at all. It was a marriage few of us could relate to from our own experience. I was married for five years; even before things became strained, my marriage was not as entwined as my parents'. They relied on each other, never stopped appreciating each other; they genuinely liked being together. A friend who is my mother's age said to me, "I've been married twice, and I never had that kind of closeness with either husband."

Shakespeare wrote plays about that kind of love; poets, songwriters, novelists, have tried to describe it. We all know about it, yet our own experiences have fallen short so many times that cynicism has taken up residence. "It would be nice, but . . ." is the most common reaction. But they have it. As a child, I felt excluded by their bond; as an adult, I'm fascinated by it. But I've never stopped puzzling over it.

As I wandered around Chasen's, it felt as if three parties had converged: a political gathering (Pete Wilson had joined that faction, as well as Colin Powell), a Hollywood party (a lot of industry talk could be heard; L.A. is ultimately a one-horse town; go to any party and you'll hear about the movie industry), and then there were my parents' friends, who were there for one purpose—to acknowledge my father's birthday.

The parking lot of Chasen's had been tented for the dinner. There was a stage with a large picture of my father as a backdrop. I thought the picture might make me sad, but it didn't. What a life he lived, I thought—it's how he would want me to see it. It was a picture taken at a state dinner years ago; he was toasting someone with a glass of champagne, smiling, with his head cocked to one side and that twinkle in his eyes that he usually had. Eighty-five years on this day—a rich life, a tender ending—except to those of us who don't want him to leave. But he would smile at that and say that everything has to end someday.

Before the dinner began, I went up to Newt Gingrich, who was sitting beside my mother. I knelt down beside his chair and said, "I want to tell you something. Even though I loathe you politically, I enjoyed spending a few minutes with you earlier, and I felt you were being quite sensitive to how difficult this evening is for my family."

I saw the word "loathe" flick across his eyes. I didn't

choose it arbitrarily; those are the kinds of feelings he evokes in many people. He listened to the rest of what I said. "I was just responding to you as a human being," he told me.

"I know. That's what struck me. And you know, that's how this nation and this world are going to change—from people responding with their hearts. Politics isn't going to change America."

"On that we agree," he said.

Feeling like I had done my part for God and country, I went back to my end of the table and watched the rest of the night unfold. There were brief speeches by Pete Wilson as well as Newt Gingrich. They were using my father so blatantly, and it seemed so unfair. But this is politics. Fairness hasn't been a part of it since the writing of the Constitution.

These men are all running for something, I thought, as Pete Wilson gave his speech; they're chasing the next election even if they don't have one coming up right away. It's the way they live their lives, define themselves; it's the only way they know. And this year, they're picking my father clean politically, running for the finish line with pounds of his flesh.

Each one talks about how Ronald Reagan changed the country, and each claims to be keeping his flame alive. Years ago, I would have listened to them talk about how my father changed America, and I'd have reacted in a judgmental, partisan way. A political way. I would have thought about the deficit, the policies I disagreed with; they weren't all good changes, I'd have grumbled. But beyond the political war zone, there are larger truths. My father did change the country; these men are right about that. But they've missed the point. He changed America because America liked him. And when we like someone, we do change; we become less rigid, more content. Even the people who disagreed with what Ronald Reagan stood for liked the man. They couldn't help it. It was his warmth, his humor.

But it was like a well-kept secret that you pass along only to certain people: "Don't tell anyone, but despite his policies, I like the guy."

Much of what he said was the stuff of myths— America, the shining city on the hill, and its people, "keepers of the American dream." He tapped into our need for myths, for visions and daydreams. Outwardly, we scoffed and called it naive—America isn't shining; she's in trouble. Carter is right. There is malaise, poverty, violence. But Carter lost because, secretly, we wanted the myth, needed it, cried out for it: "Don't tell anyone, but that shining-city-on-the-hill stuff? Sounds great—what if it could happen?" He asked us to consider that it could.

When I was a child, we drove out to the ranch on Saturdays. My father would point up to the phone lines and say, "Through all those wires, people are having conversations. Lives are being lived. Just imagine . . ."

And I did—so much so that, after a while, I thought I could hear some of those conversations.

In 1987, in a speech, my father said, "The dreams of ordinary people reach to astonishing heights. If we diplomatic pilgrims are to achieve equal altitudes, we must build all we do on the full breadth of humanity's will and consent and the full expanse of the human heart."

No one else talked to us like that. Carter didn't talk about altitudes, heights; he kept our eyes at ground level.

Mondale didn't emphasize the human heart; he told us to tighten our belts.

A friend said to me that in some of the most dramatic moments of the eighties, no one could have handled it better than my father did. The *Challenger* disaster, the bombing of the barracks in Lebanon. We felt his pain, his grief—they were real, not assembled for the camera. And—this friend said—his shoulders were big enough for us to cry on. He comforted us, but he also made us feel confident that we could go on after the astronauts died in front of us, after the boys came out in body bags.

America emerged from the seventies having had so much therapy, so much rehab, so many recovery groups, that we were sick of ourselves. We had little humor left; it was scattered behind us in various support groups and therapy sessions. Carter confronted us with our malaise. We knew he was right, but we didn't really want to hear it. We wanted to feel better, believe in bright tomorrows. Ronald Reagan provided that. Carter told us we had reason to be fearful. My father was fearless—he took a bullet and made a joke as he walked into the hospital; he recovered from that near-fatal wound with no bitterness toward the man who tried to kill him. Suddenly, in the eighties, we considered fearlessness as an option. We believed Jimmy Carter's bleak perspective; in 1984, we believed Mondale's warnings. But we wanted to believe in Ronald Reagan's shimmering vision of a better place. The guy on the white horse won.

But he also mystified us. Where was the angst? The suffering? The delusions of ego?

He mystified many people, including me. When he was shot in 1981, I thought, before I knew he would live, What if he dies? I'll never know who my father really is—on the deeper levels, the still waters that my own turbulent ways have kept me from. I have come to know him better now, as he is leaving this life, drifting farther away, than I did in the earlier years.

To understand Ronald Reagan, you have to understand the small town he came from—the ordinariness of it, planted in the sturdy, flat terrain of the Midwest, where the seasons are important, and kids dream beyond the loneliness, beyond all those endless miles, to the cities where dreams are supposed to come true. Movies provided the stories, the hopes—you could go to Hollywood and make it. I asked my mother recently how my father could have come through the Hollywood system, with all its cutthroat ways, and the political system, which is even worse, with his innocence still intact. Her answer led me back to his aloneness (he would never have considered it loneliness). He never really participated in the Hollywood lifestyle, she told me. He didn't go out with his fellow actors after a day of shooting, didn't hang out, have a few drinks. He did his work and left. He kept his dreams alive, and his innocence, by never giving too much away, by holding enough of himself in reserve so that no one could tarnish what he held dear.

He mystified the people who worked with him. They loved his sunniness, his optimism, but they didn't understand it. They've all tried to explain him—Jim Baker, Robert McFarlane, Don Regan—men who are not without guile, who are not strangers to meanness, who see it as a tool. They have talked about my father's kindness, his faith in people. But all of them end up shaking their heads slowly—they can't really explain him. When my mother would try to tell my father about this man's duplicity, or that one's conniving leaks to the press, he wouldn't believe her. In Peggy Noonan's book, *What I Saw at the Revolution,* she quoted Don Regan as saying, "The people around the president used him like you wouldn't believe. History will tell the story." History is still being written, and people are still using Ronald Reagan. But Don Regan couldn't explain my father's niceness; it allowed people to use him, but where did it come from? How did it endure?

He was the son of a shoe salesman who drank too much and a devout woman who lived by the Bible and the Golden Rule and expected her two boys to do the same. He was a quiet, nearsighted kid whose imagination stretched beyond his small, unscenic town, who wanted to get out the way kids from small towns always do. He wasn't supposed to make it. You wouldn't have bet on his succeeding; he had no connections, little money; he washed dishes to put himself through college and life-guarded at the river during the summers. You'd have laughed if someone said he would someday be president. Middle America breeds dreamers. It's the isolation of all that vastness—the wide, flat miles, the life that changes little from one generation to the next. But some make it. He did. He credited God and the faith his mother instilled in him, and he didn't analyze it much more than that. But there are clues. One of them lies in the Golden Rule—something his mother believed in, emphasized. We all grew up learning it, but few of us resolved to live it. Somewhere along the line, my father decided that it was a good way to live his life, doing unto others as he would have them do unto him. He put it into practice, wore it comfortably because it made life sweeter, an easier ride.

There is something else about the Midwest and those small towns—there is a pioneer spirit that is quintessentially American. It's the quest to ride over the next hill to a new life, a place of more possibilities. It's the "go West, young man" drive of those who know that if they stay where they are, their hopes will die. He came west, to Hollywood, to the glitter of the lights, to the soundstages and the fake cowboys and painted backdrops. It's so corny, you can't help but be swept up in the story. Because he did make it—the dream was realized. So how could he not be optimistic? How could he not be grateful when so much had gone right? He thought of himself as an example of what can happen if you dream big and persevere. He was competitive—my mother reminded me of that. He never wanted to come in second. But he never thought you had to be mean to come in first. He was proof that nice guys don't finish last. Their victories might take a little longer—remember the unsuccessful 1976 campaign when Ford won the convention? But victory did finally come, and Ronald Reagan didn't stop being a nice guy.

# MARCH 1996

When I was in seventh grade, I chose as my science project the human heart. My choice necessitated the purchase of a plastic kit which, when assembled, would be a replica of the heart; it came complete with a receptacle that was to be filled with water and red food dye. At completion, the red liquid would flow through this plastic model in the same way blood flows through a real heart.

My father helped me assemble it and built for me a three-sided wooden box in which to mount the finished product. My memory is that most of our work took place outside, in the carport and in the turnaround at the top of our steep driveway, near the rosebushes and the tree I loved to climb. There was sawing and nailing and occasional mishaps with the red-stained water; it was an outdoor project. My memory is also that it was autumn, with deep blue skies and crisp air, and that I had a sweater buttoned up over my navy-blue school uniform. I don't know if that part is an accurate memory or just the brush my imagination chose to paint with when recalling those afternoons, but it doesn't matter—in my memory, those days are deep blue and as autumnal as California ever gets.

My father never minded helping either me or my brother with such things; in fact, he looked forward to them. He was good with his hands and with tools; he liked building things, having projects to focus on. He had a habit of whistling softly while he was concentrating on whatever task his hands were occupied with. Occasionally, he whistled tunes, but sometimes it was just a sound drifting out into the late-afternoon quiet of our southern California neighborhood. The air in Los Angeles was silkier then, and the neighborhoods were quieter; they rolled into evening with the sounds of kids riding skateboards or bikes, with mothers calling out names into the sinking light, peering into the shadows for their children, whistling for pets who had wandered into someone else's yard.

We worked on my science project when I got home from school. My father did most of it—patiently, thoroughly, enjoying each stage of it. When it came time to fill up the receptacle with red water, when we opened the clamp on the tube and sent the stuff flowing through the heart like a determined river, my work began—my learning.

As I labeled the parts of the heart—the aorta, the right and left atria, the right and left ventricles—my father talked me through it, and in the process taught me to stand in awe of this small organ. Look at how perfectly designed it is, he would say, as we watched the red liquid move through the chambers, because of course we'd hooked it up correctly, and it was flowing as it should. Look at the miracle of it—so simple, yet it keeps us alive; he was, at that point, more mesmerized by our accomplishment than I was. But I watched it along with him until, unable to resist, I pressed down on the clamp and stopped the flow of our red-food-dye blood. The heart became a half-empty pool.

"Well," my father said. "I guess we lost the patient."

I opened the clamp again and brought it back to life. It seemed so simple—the blood flows through the heart and everything is fine; stop the flow and life is ended.

He taught me how the heart works, but he didn't tell me everything. He didn't tell me how to make it stop hurting. He didn't tell me if the blood slows down with the weight of sorrow. Does it turn muddy like a stream laden with debris? Is that what makes the heart feel heavy? We sat in the coppery light of those fall days and looked at a perfectly constructed mock-up of a heart. I watched it with increasing wonder and respect for its efficiency. The real version was beating in my chest; maybe my hand went to my own heart, checking on its rhythm, understanding its blood flow. I didn't know then that it could ache so.

On your way to losing a loved one, you pick up pieces of your own life and examine them differently—with a slower eye, a more delicate hand—even the moments you're living right then. I looked up from my work today and noticed how the afternoon sun was shining across the leaves of a plant that sits by the window. There was something so clean and golden about the light, I couldn't turn my eyes away. If I knew my time here was short, if I felt death reaching out for me, would I look at the sunlight on green and think, God, I'll miss that? Is that what my father thinks—deep inside him in those places that have been made remote by a disease that conquers more of him each day? I find myself looking at things the way I think he must—somewhere far below the words he can't find.

The snow is melting now in the park, revealing spots of green—stunning in their contrast to the dull, skeletal winter trees and brown slush of snow and mud in other spots. If you knew you were going to die soon—that old query that passes down through generations—what would you do with your remaining time? I would look longer at the green patches, at the few struggling buds on the bare trees, at the late-afternoon sun spilling across the leaves of a potted plant. And I would loosen my grip, lighten my touch on everyone and everything. That's what you do when someone else is leaving, when you know death is coming for a loved one—you lighten your touch. Especially if it's a parent. You have to, because people die in many ways, in many parts of themselves. They get more fragile. Sorrow can do that, too. I hold both my parents' hands more loosely now, aware of the delicacy of the bones, the soft way their hands rest on a surface. My father's hands—the hands that built fences at the ranch, jumps for the horses, science projects for his children— now feel like small birds when I hold them in mine. My mother's hands tremble these days from the stress of waiting for an end she dreads. I'm conscious of not bearing down too hard or squeezing too tightly.

One day, I looked down at my hand holding my mother's. Hers was pale, slender, fragile looking; mine was sturdy, a hand that's gardened, repaired fences, that lifts weights and works out on punching bags. I have a writer's bump on one finger and a scar on another. I loosened my hold on her hand, afraid I might be unaware of my own strength.

I T   W O U L D   B E   too simplistic to say that watching
my parents age is the reason that I've increased my
workout regime to a level that's more grueling than it is
sane; it would also be dishonest to say one has nothing to
do with the other. We watch time etch itself into our parents' faces and look for it in our own. We run farther, train
harder, to hold back the years. I'm as frightened of aging
and death as most people; the other day, I found a gray
hair and promptly plucked it out, certain that it was a
mutant growth that had sprouted by mistake and that no
others would dare follow.

But it's more than fear of aging that propels me, on
some days, to ice-skate for an hour, lift weights for another
hour, and, later in the day, run five miles. I'm getting
through this time in my family's life by keeping myself in
that peculiar Zen-like state that only an overabundance of
endorphins can create. Talk to people who have run a
marathon, or look into the eyes of those who have just finished running all those miles. They're in an altered
state—athletes know about it—it's a certain kind of calm,
a sense of floating, an evenness. And it helps. It files down
the edges of grief—the edges that sometimes feel jagged,
serrated. I watch my father's struggle with this life and my
mother's struggle to envision life without him, and a
feeling of helplessness comes over me that is so intense I
think it will rip me open. So I run, I box, I train, I skate; I
do as much as I have to, as much as my body will endure,
to smooth down the edges of the pain.

When my father was recovering from being shot, he
embarked on a self-imposed weight-lifting routine that

was so successful my mother finally begged him to slow down; he was growing out of his shirts. He was shot in the chest; he built up his musculature around the area of injury. I smiled at her frustration at having to replace an entire wardrobe of shirts, but I smiled more at what he was doing. I understood it. More than his body was being strengthened, and somewhere within him, although he never would have admitted it, fears were being smoothed out, calmed. He had to face people again, walk out unafraid, not be crippled by memories of a boy with a gun aimed right at him.

These days he sleeps—with the same fervor, the same determination—deeply, as if waking up were something he hadn't considered. Last night I dreamed that I slept so soundly and so long that, when I woke, an entire day had passed by. For the remainder of the dream I was chasing down every clock I could find, trying to prove that I hadn't really lost a whole day.

Our parents' passages become entwined in our own. Under a gray sky, with the sun struggling through the clouds, I ran through the park this morning, listening to the sound of my feet on the asphalt, feeling the cold air in my lungs. In my dream, I slept as my father does now; in my daily life, I do what he used to do—turn my body into a metaphor for my emotions, make it stronger, more capable. Along the way, I try to notice the small things— the bright green moss tucked into crevices of gray rock, the first buds about to open on the trees—the things I would miss if I were leaving this earth soon.

## APRIL 1996

"I'm not as scared anymore; I just know I'll be so lonely without him."

They were my mother's words, the night before Easter, as I watched a red sun sink into the river from my twelfth-floor apartment. The lights of Lincoln Center came on as the sky kept re-creating itself; there was a streak of white cloud across one half and orange ribbons across the other, over the spot where the sun sank. Shades of purple came and went, and darkness was moving in steadily.

It all seemed laced together at that moment—Easter, celebrating the Resurrection of Jesus; my mother's words, revealing her willingness to move past her fear; and the sun, setting as it always has, as it always will, no matter who dies or who is born.

I've thought more about Easter and Passover this year than ever before. Moses—the lonely, dedicated man whose only friend was God—and Jesus, proving to his followers that death isn't really an ending. My mother and I stayed on the phone until the sky—at my end of the country—had surrendered to darkness. We talked about faith, and God, and death. We talked about how far my father has disappeared into this illness. We had both watched the same program on Moses the night before, and my mother said, "It seemed so mean of God to not let Moses into the Promised Land after all those years and all that faith." I knew what she was thinking because I wrestle with the same thoughts—how do you hold on to faith when it seems that God is being unkind?

My father's doctor called my mother earlier and apologized for having been unable to come to the house for the past two weeks. He's had a cold and didn't want to risk exposing either of my parents. Then he said, "I see a lot of patients with Alzheimer's and other neurological conditions that are similar. I watch them degenerate, slip away. But seeing your husband slip away affects me so deeply. I feel depressed when I leave your house; it's just so sad."

This web of sorrow and of prayers is spun by so many different people—my father's doctor, a woman who attends my parents' church who called to say that her prayer group is praying for him. But in the end, God will decide how long he stays, how bad things will get. We do our part, but we are witnesses. My mother and I talked about the language of prayers.

"Do you remember a story your father used to tell about when he played football?" she said. "He would pray before every game, and for a while he thought he was the only one. Then gradually he learned that most of the other guys were praying as well. He realized he couldn't pray to win because the other team wanted to win also, and everyone was equal in God's eyes. So he prayed that no one would get hurt and that everyone would play the best they could. He left the rest up to God."

"That's what we have to do," I told her.

"I know. It's just so difficult to watch this progress."

"You have a huge responsibility in this. He needs you to release him, but if he senses your fear, he won't want to go. The two of you are so close that he'll know intuitively if you're scared."

That's when she said, "I'm not as scared anymore; I just know I'll be so lonely without him."

Some part of me breathed easier, let go a little, as if that part had been holding its breath. I wondered again if my mother would choose to not stay in a world without my father. It's a fear that's stayed inside me, that I've offered up in prayers, hoping for a sign, an answer. But the only answer is that I have to trust in God's wisdom. People write their own stories, set the timing on their lives and their deaths in ways that often defy explanation.

My father told me once, a long time ago, that in the Korean War some men got so despondent, so fed up with living, that they crawled under their blankets and stayed there until, days later, they were found dead. He said they gave it a name—"give-up-itis." There was no physical cause for their deaths—they just didn't want to live. I don't know if that's a true story or a made-up war story, and it doesn't matter. Things like that happen.

My parents are entwined; it's a deep, mysterious bond. I was born from it, yet I float outside it. I could never stand in the way if they wanted to remain together. The flow of their passion is beyond my reach; it always will be.

We don't choose whom we love, nor do we control how deep that love will be. Love finds us, and we're swept along; we either go kicking and screaming or we go will-

ingly, but always we are humbled, awestruck by the un-
bridled power of the heart. We reach out with a fury we
didn't know we had—to save the people we love, to hold
them, to carry them, sometimes to release them. And we
reach inward, trying to make sense of it. At one time or
another, we're driven to our knees. Over this Easter
weekend, the images of Moses reaching up to the heavens
for guidance, or falling to his knees in prayer, have followed me, tugged at me. I thought of my mother kneeling
down to pray one night and getting lost in a flood of tears.
That was when my fear started—when she told me that.
Somewhere in her tears was a prayer. What was it? That
God would take her, too? Or did she ask for the strength
to stay behind? I didn't ask. Prayers are the purest of
secrets; they can be shared but not intruded upon, offered
but not commanded.

It was dark when we finished talking. My mother had
to pack; she was taking a morning flight to New York,
where she planned to stay for a few days. I hung up the
phone but kept her voice in my ear, playing back the
words that gave me hope. Maybe she will choose to face an
unwieldy future, tackle the hollow of loneliness, stay here
awhile longer.

EASTER SUNDAY FELT like winter. Rain began
in the morning and lasted all day. I knew I wouldn't be
talking to my mother because she would be traveling and
wouldn't get to New York until late.

I thought about the absence of her voice—studied it,
lingered with it, as the day stretched on and the rain fell.

No ringing phone would have her on the other end, unless she called from the plane, which I've never known her to do. I couldn't dial a number and reach her. I imagined the silence stretching out beyond that one day. What if it was permanent? What if my parents' love for each other is a cord that can't loosen or stretch, and they're meant to remain bound in death as they have been in life? Would I be able to forgive God for silencing both their voices? For leaving me with the vastness of their absence and the weight of all the years when I was so arrogant I didn't think I needed them?

My mother has only recently come into my life; we're still learning about each other. I don't feel restricted in what I tell her, and she fills me with stories and memories that can't come from anyone else. If it ended, if I was no longer anyone's daughter, would I rail at God or trust in his compassion?

By late afternoon, I had to stop exploring these thoughts; the pain was too great.

ON MONDAY EVENING, my mother and I had an early dinner and then called my father from her hotel room. She told him about the unseasonably cold weather, the prediction for snow the next day. She told him she would be back soon and that she loved him. I don't know what his responses were; often these days he just listens. When she handed the phone to me, I told him it was great skating weather. It's still one passageway into his memory—skating, the river, those long, icy winters. "I've learned to skate backward," I told him.

"Oh, that's good," he said, and I could hear him reaching for the words. "Learning to skate backward is something that's welcome."

His sweetness fills in the gaps, colors over the words that don't quite fit.

When my mother and I said goodnight, she held on to me tightly. I could feel her starting to cry. "I love spending time with you so much," she said.

"Me, too," I told her, feeling the soft exhalation inside me again, the hope that this will be enough to make her want to stay, to let the cord unravel—just a little—from my father, trusting that it will still be around them, that they won't really be that far away from each other.

## APRIL 1996, LOS ANGELES

Early on a Saturday morning, my mother and I left for the ranch my parents have owned since 1974. During my father's presidency, it was known as the Western White House. It's north of Santa Barbara, at the top of a mountain—six hundred and eighty-eight acres of hills, tall oak trees, and sweeping vistas. There is one spot along a high trail where you can look down at the Pacific Ocean on one side and the Santa Ynez Valley on the other. It was my father's favorite spot.

My mother wanted to clean some things out of the ranch house. They don't go there anymore; my father's world has become smaller—a typical symptom of Alzheimer's—and it's disorienting for him to travel two hours by car to a place that's slipping from his memory.

Over the past twenty-two years, I have seen this land in rain, in brilliant, startling sunlight; I've driven up the winding mountain road in thick fog, and in the dry, crackling months of summer. But I haven't been back in a long time, and this time its beauty took my breath away. Not because the land had changed, but because I had. In other years, I had trouble seeing beyond whatever resentments stood between me and my parents; my heart was too small, too self-involved to really take in the beauty that was around me.

It was late morning when we drove through the gates of the ranch—Rancho del Cielo—a perfect name for this land that seems so close to the sky. The morning was overcast, and there was a strong wind. The hills were green from recent rains, covered by a blanket of long grasses— the wind gliding across them created silken waves that hypnotized the eye.

My father's spirit was everywhere, in the things he built with his own hands—the fencing around the house, built from telephone poles; the dock at the pond; even the pond itself. It's a natural pond, but it used to dry up in summer. So he lined the bottom with plastic, bought tiny goldfish at Sears, and now the runoff from the hills fills it, and it stays full all year. The goldfish are huge. Weeping willows, which he planted from cuttings, bend gracefully over the water.

But as much as his presence is still felt there, so is his absence. I heard it in the sound of the wind—a lonely echo—as I sat on a steep hillside drinking in the beauty around me, looking down at the house with smoke curling up from the chimneys. Fireplaces are the only source of heat in the small, two-bedroom house, and my father was always cutting firewood. But he never cut down a tree. He got wood from trimming the lower branches on the oaks and the madrones, which he would have done anyway because he liked to ride under the trees.

I saw his absence—felt it—in the empty tack room; all the saddles are gone. And in the empty fields—there are still some hoofprints embedded in the earth, but the horses have been given away. There used to be a few cows and two Texas longhorns—Duke and Duchess. Duke died, and now Duchess roams the property alone, grazing, lying in the sun, but with no companion, no herd. I saw her several times during the day, and she came to symbolize the loneliness that has settled onto this land my father loved so much.

Duke is buried in the animal graveyard that my father started for the animals who had reached the end of their lives, after long years in what must have seemed like paradise to them. My dog is buried there—Freebo, the dog I had before Sadie—whom I raised in Topanga Canyon with more freedom than a dog in the city could ever have. When I left the canyon, I tried to turn him into a city dog, but he was miserable. He lived the rest of his years on the ranch, chasing squirrels and birds and following my father on horseback rides. Other dogs are buried there; all of them lived long lives. The horse my mother used to ride is there, too. They all have stone markers with their names and dates painted on them. My father picked the spot—on a hill that's shaded by oak trees. One tree arches over the slope where the animals are buried.

He didn't want to tamper too much with nature. It would be difficult to bury a large animal like a horse or a cow, so he came up with a solution that he felt fit into the cycle of things. When Duke was too ill to go on, and my mother's horse had reached the end of his life, they were taken to a remote end of the property and euthanized there. Then my father, feeling that "nature should take its course," left their bodies for the birds and animals who live because others die; a few weeks later, he would go out, collect the bones, and bury them under the oak tree.

The harshness of death didn't bother him—it was part of the cycle.

The future of the ranch is uncertain. It's an ongoing expense and is hardly used now. It's painful for my mother to go there; she never spends the night, never walks the trails or sits by the pond. Memories are everywhere. She does what she needs to do and leaves.

I sat on the hillside after the sun had come out and the day had turned golden, and I could feel the ranch slipping away from me—the land that's so infused with my father's spirit. Life these days feels like a litany of goodbyes; the idea that this could be another cut into my heart.

The solution would be so easy, so simple, I thought, if I were wealthy. I could take over the payments or just buy the property—bring horses back to it, get some cows to keep Duchess company. My thoughts stepped onto a shaky platform then—what if? It's always futile, a night train to regrets and unrequited wishes, judgments about time wasted and paths not taken. What if I hadn't made so many wrong choices in my life? What if I'd been smarter in my career, accepted some of the acting jobs I turned down in the early eighties when my father had just been elected and I was the flavor of the month? Acting is the only thing I know how to do other than write, and at that point I was supporting myself as an actress—but I turned down some bad parts for big money. In retrospect, I was a fool. I could be more successful now, richer, be in a position to take over the ranch and manage it the way my father had. I could carry on his legacy, use what he taught me about the land and nature. There is nothing I would do differently with the ranch. He taught me to respect both the harmony and the harshness of nature. Vultures and buzzards feed off the bodies of dead animals because it's how they survive. Rattlesnakes have their place in the scheme of things; you watch for them, listen for them, make a wide path around them, but you don't kill them unless it's an extraordinary situation in which an animal or a person is in danger. There are few fences at the ranch. The cows and horses wandered the acreage, the horses always preferring the pasture near the house. They were allowed to establish their own boundaries.

Ultimately, after my dark ride on the "what if" train, I carried a piece of my father's legacy inside me as we left the ranch and drove back to Los Angeles with an orange sun sinking into the Pacific. My mother and I were both lost in our own thoughts.

People leave their footprints on this earth by what they leave behind—the bits and pieces of who they were, of what they learned, accomplished, created. Often it's through their children. They lay threads at their children's feet, hoping their sons or daughters will choose one and continue weaving the rope that binds one generation to another. But it's never certain which thread children will choose, or if they will choose any at all.

I saw, in the acres of land spread out around me, in the windblown grasses and the sun bathing the hills, the thread I wanted to pick up, the rope I wanted to continue weaving, the legacy my father had instilled in me during long afternoons on horseback and jeep rides along steep trails.

There is a secret thought that the offspring of famous people keep tucked away. It becomes the focal point of our lives, although it takes years to see that. It's what makes us run from who we are, rage against the huge shadow we feel dwarfed by, sabotage ourselves again and again. We vilify anyone who suggests we have a legacy to live up to, shoes to fill, a torch to carry. Because underneath it all, deep inside us, we think they're right. The thought infuriates us, terrifies us, but also haunts us with a gentle, constant pressure. It can't have been random, we think, this anointed life we were born into. We grow up so close to power—mesmerized by it, blanketed by it, yet confused; our resentment mounts until we think our very survival depends on separating ourselves from the parent whose shadow falls so large over us. But the thought won't go away: What if there is a reason for our genealogy? What if we have a responsibility that we're not living up to?

We suspect there might have been a private transaction between souls, long before our birth, when we were asked to accept the inheritance of a larger-than-life parent, and we said yes. But we ravage the best years of our lives, screaming out, No! I'm my own person—separate, unconnected to this shadow, this father or mother who has left such a large imprint on the world. We compose outlaw lives, but we're still plagued by the thought that we're denying our true selves.

I remember, in 1964, sitting in an auditorium in Arizona listening to my father give a speech for Barry Goldwater. I was twelve years old, and already some ideas were forming in my head that differed from the political ideology I heard at home. The words and ideas of my father's speech are not what I remember about that night; my disagreements, young as I was, were just some errant thoughts floating through my mind. What I remember is being overwhelmed by my father's ability to hold an audience mesmerized, to move them, bring them to tears or have them leaping to their feet. I wanted to do that. It was almost intoxicating, dreaming of having that ability, wishing that it could someday be passed to me—a precious torch, lit so it could be handed down. Of course, I had no idea what I would say if I were behind the podium; I didn't even know who would be up there. Which is the struggle that most children of famous people go through: we're chased down by a nagging thought about the responsibility of our legacy, but we have to figure out who we are before we can possibly know what to inherit. It sends us into crazy tailspins, makes us reinvent ourselves constantly, searching desperately for ourselves. The answer is in our bloodstreams, our hearts—we are our parents' children, and somewhere in that tangled history is a thread that's waiting to be found.

My political ideology never moved any closer to my father's, but just as I followed him on horseback, imitating his posture, his elegant way of sitting in the saddle, I followed his instruction about preserving the harmony of the land, letting "nature take its course." I never doubted any of it; it always felt true.

What I found, during that afternoon at the ranch, was the strongest link between me and my father, the one that had never been shredded by doubts. When I told a friend about wishing I could take over the ranch, he said, "You have to envision yourself there—hold that image in your mind."

"You mean like, 'If you build it, he will come'?" I asked.

"Exactly like that," he answered.

• • •

MY FATHER IS getting smaller. He's over six feet tall, or he used to be. Even at five feet, ten inches, I had to tilt my face up to look at him, stand on my tiptoes when I hugged him. Now I look straight ahead into his eyes, and my feet stay firmly planted when we hug. His legs are thinner; they're no longer the muscular legs of an athletic man. But it's more than his physical body. It's his personality, his essence—the comforting, familiar qualities we put under the heading of "character" or "identity" because we don't know what else to call them, and people mystify us more than we admit. He's being whittled down, trimmed, reshaped by a disease that has its own blueprint.

When I was a very young child, I had a blanket that I carried with me everywhere. I slept with it, clutched it throughout the day, and screamed if anyone tried to remove it from my hand. It was named Blankie. My parents began to wonder if I would ever let it go and spoke to the pediatrician about how to wean me from my ever-present blanket. He suggested trimming it down gradually—taking scissors to it and making it smaller every few days so that eventually I would lose interest in it. Obediently, my parents followed his advice, but with disappointing results. When the blanket had been reduced to the size of a dish towel, I was still clutching it constantly. So they cut it down even more, to the measurements of a washcloth, at which point—according to my parents—I said, "One day, Blankie will be gone completely, won't it?"

My father is being reduced by a force beyond anyone's control. I wonder sometimes if we are clutching to him in ways that we're not even aware of, holding him here.

His doctor came to my parents' house to see him on an afternoon when I was there, and he asked me if I had noticed a progression of the disease.

"I have," I admitted, "but more than that I think he's torn between wanting to leave and wanting to stay." I elaborated on this, noticing, as I continued, the doctor's brow furrowing, his eyes looking at me as if I were speaking in tongues.

"He can't reason that way," he finally said. "With Alzheimer's, the neurons that allow someone to make choices like that are dying. He can feel emotionally, but conscious choice . . ."

I tried to explain that I wasn't talking about his neurons—I wasn't even talking about his brain. "I mean his soul," I told him. But as far as the doctor was concerned, I was still speaking in tongues.

I think I'm right, though. And I feel guilty if we are keeping him here—this family that was so fractured and has finally learned to get along. We caused him pain at times, baffled him at others. My father is a simple man. What was he to do with a daughter who adopted as her role models every poet who either committed suicide or thought about it? I idolized Sylvia Plath—her head in the oven, her poems reading like litanies to death. I used to mail my poetry to my parents when I was away at high school. My father, the sunniest of men, for whom optimism is a natural state of being, was bewildered at my darkness. He shrugged off life's shadows; I chased them down, adopted them, and filled notebooks with them.

What was he to do with a son whose intellectual

curiosity and studious rationalism created a twelve-year-old who liked to discuss the Eastern concept of Nirvana and who used words like "ethos" and "nihilistic"? When Ron was tiny, our father dubbed him "Happy Jack." I can imagine him wondering, When did my son become so analytical—an armchair philosopher before he's even passed through puberty?

Two Christmases ago, our father looked at Maureen and said, "I remember a little blond girl announcing that she was going to run away from home. She started walking out the door with her coat and her doll."

"And you gave me a dollar and told me to call when I found a job," Maureen said.

His eyes twinkled. "Well, it worked," he said. "You came back pretty quick."

This is the story: When my father and Jane Wyman, Maureen's mother, were still married, they lived on a quiet, residential street, up a steep driveway. When Maureen announced her intention to run away, our father knew that talking her out of it wouldn't work. So he played along, gave her a dollar, and they watched their tiny daughter walk down the driveway. She stood out on the street, looking in both directions, waiting, probably, for someone to come down the hill and get her. When no one did, she went back, walked into the house, and said, "I'm back."

My father always knew what to do with his children's problems and dramas when we were still small. A child planning to run away was simple to deal with. But many years later, after Maureen was physically abused by her first husband, she ran to the YWCA to escape him, not telling our father what had happened until later. It's another kind of running away—an older version—and I don't know if he understood it.

Michael's gratitude at having been adopted as a baby, folded into the Reagan family, has presented our father with more emotion than he is comfortable dealing with. It took me a long time to realize my father's shyness. It makes him back away from emotions that seem huge to him—not because he isn't affected by them, but because he is, and that makes him self-conscious.

At times, we have all left him perplexed, overwhelmed. But we have grown up, grown calmer, and have come home to attend his departure. That's his dilemma— he's waited so long to see us like this, to experience us as a family. His eyes move over us when we are all together— taking in what he has longed to see. And then his gaze travels to some obscure point in the distance, as if he's weighing his choices.

# MAY 1996

My father went to the Reagan Library the other day—a plan that, when I first heard about it, elicited a response of "He's going where?" I thought, What if he's not having a good day? There are always visitors to the library; visions of strangers trying to engage him in conversation immediately sprang into my mind, made me react protectively.

But he went—unannounced, accompanied by Secret Service agents and one of his "caregivers," a word I never used before Alzheimer's entered our lives. Part of the initiation into the world of disease is an introduction to a new vocabulary. Sadly, it becomes a link to others who wander around in this strange, defeated territory.

Obviously, my father did not go unnoticed as he walked through the library, but no one intruded or tried to get into a dialogue with him. There is a five-minute film that people can look at when they first enter; it's a Cliffs Notes version of my father's life. On this day, he sat down to watch it as if he were just another visitor. My mother was told later that tears welled up in his eyes as he looked at the images of his life on the screen. Was it longing for the life he's lived? Sorrow that life passes so quickly? Maybe it was the flutter of some deep, mysterious dream that he never shared with anyone. It's impossible to know.

I haven't been to the library yet . . . not because I haven't had opportunities. With all my trips back to Los Angeles, I could have taken half a day to drive to Simi Valley, where the Reagan Library sits on top of a hill, surrounded by trees. My reluctance is something I haven't entirely figured out, but I'm beyond denying that reluctance is exactly what sits inside me like an immovable stone. The library, like other presidential libraries, is more of a museum, with exhibits, short films, displays encased in glass.

There is something about the dismantling of a person's life—the cataloguing of it—that tears at me, makes me want to turn away. I feel as if I'm rifling through drawers or peering into a closet when the door has been left ajar. The organization of museums is artificial; people's lives are messy, tumultuous—they don't fall into alphabetical order.

It cuts deeper when it's my father's life that has been organized into a tour, a chronological journey with exhibits meant to give insight into him as a human being. People come to the Reagan Library hoping to know the man better, hoping to drift across an invisible boundary line and enter his life. I realize it's as close as they can come to knowing him; I appreciate that they want to.

But you still won't know him, I want to say. You can look at his saddles, but you can't see the joy and serenity on his face when he would get on his horse and ride along trails at the ranch. You can't hear him soothe a frightened horse with the soft stream of his voice. You can't see his hand reach down to pat his horse's sturdy neck—the hand with a dent in the thumb from a childhood accident when his brother swung an ax at him. You can look at his English riding boots, stained with horse's sweat and scuffed on the heels. But you can't smell the pungent scent of horse's sweat on leather. I could tell you that that scent was sweeter than any perfume to me when I was young; it came from long afternoons on horseback, riding with my father. I could tell you, but I can't take you back to those days. You can't know how hollow the tack room feels now with all the empty racks that once held saddles, the naked hooks where bridles used to hang.

My mother has told me that at the library there is a picture of my father as a young lifeguard. You can stand in front of it, admire his youth, his tan, athletic body. But you can't see the way his eyes sparkled decades later when he told stories about rescuing city boys who tried to impress their girlfriends with their swimming ability and got caught in currents they couldn't handle. He was never unkind when he told these stories; he just found their bravado amusing.

A friend who has been to the library told me there is a picture of the Rock River there. "You'd like seeing it," he said. "You've written about your father ice-skating on it."

I will eventually see that photograph. But I've already seen the river—my father made it come to life by describing its wide, watery passage as it snaked through farmland on its way to the Mississippi. It was "blue-green in the summer, surrounded by wooded hills and limestone cliffs," he said. And in the winter when it froze, "it was a skating rink as wide as two football fields and as long as I wanted to make it."

Behind photographs are silent stories. You could stand in front of a picture of the Rock River for hours and not hear those stories. They need my father's voice, his eyes, his way of breathing life into memories.

I know also that there is a picture of his childhood home in Dixon, Illinois—a small, plain, two-story house. But you might not know that in the upstairs bedroom was a shy, nearsighted boy, small for his age, reading every book he could find on birds and wildlife. He read *Northern Lights,* a book about the white wolves of the North, again and again; he imagined himself running wild with the wolves across snowy fields, up to steep cliffs, and down through shadowy ravines.

Whatever my hesitation has been about visiting the library, I will have to set it aside—I know that. It's a part of our lives and will become a bigger part. My parents will be buried there. I learned about this a few years ago, when I was still estranged from my family and news about them came only from newspapers and the evening news. They had to get some sort of special permission to be buried at the library; I suppose there are zoning restrictions on where people can be buried. I remember picturing two burial plots, two headstones, up on a hilltop—with no others for miles around. It felt lonely to me, isolated; I had the strange thought that, in a cemetery, there is some sort of companionship between the spirits floating around and between the people who come to grieve. But my parents' lives have always wrapped around each other with little need for anyone else. So maybe it's fitting that they will be laid to rest on a high hilltop, together as they were in life, a bit distant from the rest of us because they were completed by each other.

Almost all of my parents' possessions will end up at the library, too. My mother told me this one afternoon as I was standing in her dressing room waiting for her to put on lipstick and comb her hair. I looked around at all the tiny porcelain and silver boxes, the silver picture frames, the crystal vases. "All of this?" I said. She nodded yes.

At first it seemed like an intrusion—people looking at their personal possessions. But then I remembered how little is personal when you've entered the public arena. There is an obligation to let people in, to allow them to feel like they know you. Things collected over a lifetime can give insight into someone, or at least give the illusion of insight.

Years ago, when I lived in Topanga Canyon in a house with a large garden, I was digging in the soil to plant my fall crop of lettuce, and I unearthed a child's shoe. It was a small leather sandal, caked with mud. I sat down with the shoe cradled in my hand and wondered about the child who had lost it. Maybe it was so long ago that the garden which was, by then, a beautiful, terraced work of love with vegetable plots and low stone walls was still a wild hillside. Maybe the child was digging for earthworms or running through high summer grasses and mustard weeds when he or she lost the shoe and couldn't find it again.

Maybe a visitor to the Reagan Library will look at one of my mother's silver boxes and wonder where she got it. They might imagine her walking on a narrow street in London, spotting it in the window of an antique store. Perhaps it was handed down, they might think, or given to her as a birthday gift. People will look at my parents' possessions and give them stories because they have to. It's a way of turning the object into a window into someone else's life.

And what story will I give to something like a silver box that once sat beside my mother's mirror on her dressing table? I don't know where it came from; I only know it will someday belong to the library, be offered to the public for viewing, as so much of our lives has been. The afternoon sun glinted across it, and it was polished so perfectly the lush trees outside the window were reflected in its surface. It was one of several, there was nothing in it, and in that moment it seemed to symbolize how much is changing in the life of my family, how much is moving on, leaving.

Change either crashes down on us unexpectedly, or it moves in slowly, inevitably, like a storm front that's holding its course. Either way, it's beyond our control. My family has a life beyond itself. We're part of history. My parents will be buried on a hilltop on the grounds of a library named for my father, full of exhibits of his life, displays of my parents' possessions. People who never met them will tour the place where they will live forever. Visitors will linger at glass cases, staring at the accumulations of a lifetime, at photographs of a time gone by. The glass is the metaphor; something is always on the other side of it, just out of reach.

MY PHONE RANG at twelve-thirty last night. Startled from sleep, I immediately thought of my father.

This is it, I thought, even before I picked up the receiver. When I heard my mother's voice on the other end, I was sure.

"Something happened with your father," she said. "I'm sorry to wake you." But her voice sounded calm. My mind was organizing itself into plane reservations, appointments I'd have to cancel, but the evenness of her tone was confusing me.

It wasn't what I feared. My father had been alone with the man who helps care for him—his other caregiver—when he suddenly asked where I was. He was told that I wasn't there, but he pointed to a chair and said, "Yes, she is. She was just sitting right there."

My mother reminded me that I have told her I believe people give signs when they are nearing the end of this life. One of the signs can be seeing the spirits of people who have already died, or who are alive but far away geographically. I think our internal vision is keener toward the end.

It wasn't surprising to me that my father thought he saw me there. For most of the day, my thoughts had been with him. I have days like that now when I feel remote, snagged by someone else's reality—his. On those days, I feel like an observer of my own life, not a participant. It was more significant that my mother called me at twelve-thirty to tell me what he had said instead of waiting until the next day. The information could have waited, but she couldn't. The loneliness of losing him must get worse at night; the dark must yawn around her like an endless black wasteland.

Anyone who has watched one parent get ill and has felt the desolation of the other parent knows what helplessness feels like. There is no way to ease their pain or lift their loneliness. The only way past those feelings is through them. So we answer the phone late at night, and we listen, and we try to say something comforting. It's never enough, but it's all we have to give.

There is something else those who have gone through this know: the days start to wear you down, wear away whatever polish you once had, the layers that protected your rawest emotions. A friend snapped at me the other night over something trivial—interrupting him, I think—and I felt a wound open up in me that was out of proportion to the incident itself. It was just a small moment in a friendship—one friend getting irritated and expressing it. But I have no layers of skin now, I thought.

At night, I open the windows in my bedroom so I can hear the traffic below me. I like to think of people in motion, going places; so much of my family's life feels stationary right now. We are holding still, waiting—often it seems like we're holding our breath. I go to sleep with the sound of movement and imagine people for whom death is a distant notion. I know the reality is much different; there are people driving in the streets below me with their own pain slowing them down. But it helps to imagine.

## July 1996, Los Angeles

My father still stands up when I come into the room, but he has to hoist himself out of the chair. Weaker now, he uses a combination of arm pressure and momentum to bring himself to his feet. When I was seventeen and had reluctantly agreed to be a debutante, I danced on his feet at the debutante ball. I didn't know how to waltz, and he said, "That's okay—just stand on my feet." It felt like floating. My father was tall and strong, and he glided around the floor with me balanced on his feet as if I weighed no more than a pair of laces. Now I hold his arm as we walk through my parents' careful living room—everything tastefully placed—and I notice his weight pressing into my hand.

He was so happy to see me when I came in. "Oh, you've come to visit me," he said, his face brightening. A moment later, he added, "Where have you been?" And I felt the now-familiar thud of pain inside me. I explained that I had been in New York and hadn't been able to fly out to L.A. for a couple of months. I wondered if he had been feeling abandoned by me. So much of our history together has been that—my walking away, turning my back on him. I don't know which experiences remain the

most vivid for him. Maybe the times I shunned him—
those long, frozen years—are still bright, prominent in his
mind. Maybe the years get jumbled—past and present
turned upside down. I try to tell him, with my eyes more
than my words, that I'm here, that I won't abandon my
family again.

Sometimes he is right there, watching and listening.
Other times, he floats off, content to drift away from us.
There's a strange beauty to it, a peacefulness. The silence
feels silken. "It's like talking to a cloud," my mother has
said of those moments. I'm not sure she realizes how
lovely that image is.

I watch him when he drifts off. When I was a child
and we would go out to the ranch, I liked to climb up on
the bales of hay in the barn and hide there. I would stretch
out on my stomach, breathe in the thick, sweet smell of
the hay, chew on a piece of it, and watch my father down
below, getting our saddles from the tack room, bridles,
grooming tools for the horses. There was a window high
up in the barn, and I remember dust particles glittering
in the yellow shaft of sunlight, the horses pawing the
ground where they were tied outside. My father went
about his tasks, whistling softly, the way he usually did,
content with his life on those long, easy afternoons. He
never whistles anymore. There have been years when we
had no contact with each other, so I don't know when he
stopped.

Now he likes to look across the garden—the green
lawn sloping down to colorful, exquisitely tended flower
beds, the city spread out in the distance. I stand beside
him, looking at him as he looks out—at sunlight bounc-

ing off white buildings so far away they seem like toys, at the mottled patches of shade beneath the trees. His eyes are paler than the sky they used to match.

"He did it well," he says, waving his hand in the direction of the city, the horizon.

"God?" I ask—guessing, reaching for what I hope is the right thread.

"Uh-huh."

"Yes, God did do a good job," I assure him, clinging to the moment.


MY MOTHER'S LIFE these days is like a garment that's being taken apart stitch by stitch. One of her closest friends—a woman she has known for decades—has died unexpectedly. She fainted on my mother's birthday. The small birthday celebration which I went to with her took on a somber tone; none of the women there knew how serious their friend's condition was, only that she had been taken to the hospital. She never regained consciousness. A massive stroke had destroyed the left side of her brain, and three days later, they took her off life support.

There was little I could say to comfort my mother. I watch the steady unraveling of the life she has lived, knowing it's going to get worse, and I resort to things like "At least she didn't suffer."

My parents' house is closed up early for night. Long before the sun has relinquished its hold on the sky, dinner is over and the drapes are drawn. Yesterday evening, I left their house, with its closed curtains, shadows, and lamp-light inside, and I went back to the beach. With hours of daylight left, I walked along the shore, through sunset and the soft, blue hour that follows—the magic hour, photographers call it. I thought of my parents heading early into night while I walk on the beach, and stay until it's almost dark, squeezing out the last moments of the day.

## July 1996

Throughout our lives, we shuffle images in our memories—as if they were a deck of cards or, more accurately, a stack of photographs. One picture ends up on top, faceup, an emblem of what we have chosen to remember. We do it with places, with events, but most often we do it with people. The image we choose varies according to where we are in our lives, who we have become, how generous or angry or philosophical we are about the person we are remembering.

When I think of my mother, the picture that comes to mind is an old one. She is coming into the yellow kitchen of our house in Pacific Palisades—the house I grew up in. She is carrying a basket of roses that she's just clipped from the bushes which line the driveway. She still has her gardening gloves on and her straw hat that shields her eyes from the sun. She is wearing slacks and a blouse and is smiling because she loves roses, loves arranging them in vases.

I don't know why this is the image that comes to me now when I think of my mother, except perhaps that it was a more innocent time. The days seemed longer. Fewer people around us were dying.

There is an image of my father that has always been

shuffled to the most prominent place in my memory. He is on horseback, looking out over the ranch he loves, the land he gets sustenance from. Over the years, the ranch he is gazing across has changed. Once, it was the land he owned when I was younger—in Agoura—with white fences around the pastures and the duck pond where I used to play in the mud and look for frogs. Now in the snapshot that my memory pulls up, he is on a hilltop at the Santa Barbara ranch, looking at the ocean in the distance, the fog inching up the side of the mountain, the clusters of oak trees. The land he is looking across may have changed, but his love for it never has; it's there in his eyes, his relaxed smile.

There are signs that my mother wants to sell the ranch—guarded comments, hints. I don't ask because if the answer is yes, I don't know if I have anywhere left to put the pain. I brought it up once—clumsily—trying to tell her that no one else should ever have that ranch. My father's presence is so strong there, I was attempting to say, but my words felt unwieldy, cumbersome, slippery with emotion. "I'll do what I have to do," she said, ending the discussion.

I know that her answer went beyond finances. It had to do with memories—of days that are painful to revisit because they rolled by so smoothly, with a peaceful laziness that awaits anyone lucky enough to escape the city and retreat into the hills. The ranch was where my father went to restore himself, and my mother settled into the long stretch of days, content to simply be with him and let the hours float by. Now those days are far behind her, out of reach. I watched her when we went to the ranch together recently. I saw how her eyes rested on the lake, the hills, but only for a moment. Then something in her raced away from her recollections. At the end of the day, she couldn't wait to leave, as if the land itself were haunted.

Maybe one of the differences between losing a parent and losing a partner, a lover, a spouse, lies in the way we handle memories. When you are losing a parent, you hoard memories, become avaricious, uncompromising. Something takes over, consumes you. The day we went to the ranch, I could have sat on a hilltop until dark, drinking in every bit of my father, every echo of him that drifted by on air currents, that rose out of the earth. I studied the fences he built from telephone poles, saw how he notched out the wood, constructing them with hardly any nails. I memorized the pattern of trails through the hills, designed to provide the best views, especially from horseback. I let myself be saturated with his presence— still strong even though he hasn't physically set foot on the ranch for many months, and probably never will again.

It seems strange at first, but in losing parents, you also find them—in places, in certain possessions. I know a girl who always wore her father's watch after he died. It was silver, bulky, not very stylish, and was too big for her. But she wore it with evening dresses, jeans, gym clothes. She needed it on her arm, refused to take it off. That's what happens—we become possessive guardians of the things or places that resonate with our parents' spirit.

But for the one whose life has been wrenched apart, who has lost his or her mate, the memories are too many, too weighty. That person is like someone drowning, forced to cast off clothing, shoes, bags—whatever has weight, because survival depends on being able to come to the surface.

Losing my father and losing the ranch have become part of the same sorrow; it's as if I will be losing him twice. And understanding my mother's motives makes it more difficult, because no one's right, and no one's wrong. It's as if something inside me is crying out, You can't sell the ranch—he's everywhere on it. And she is responding by crying out, That's why I have to.

Maybe it comes down to this: For me, that land is fertile, rich with my father's presence. I want to water it, nurture it, keep it alive. For my mother, it's fallow—a reminder of the life she has lost, the life that's dying. She wants to leave it behind. There is nothing there for her now.

# AUGUST 1996

There is a rock along a trail at the ranch that my father dubbed "Heart Rock." Not because of the shape of the rock—it's actually a shallow cave—but because he painted all of our initials on its flat inner surface, with hearts around them.

In a dense patch of trees, there is one he called Hangman's Tree—an appropriate name because there are notches along one of the branches, made by ropes that did, a long time ago, have bodies dangling from them. The land that is now called Rancho del Cielo was not always an idyllic place; the war known as the settling of America was fought, in part, on these acres. On some of the surrounding ranches, there are Indian caves and, I'm sure, other hanging trees or similar reminders that this country was not settled peacefully.

There is another story to the ranch. My mother and father bought it from the parents of a high school friend of mine who was killed in a New Year's Eve auto accident years ago.

Glenda Cornelius was to have inherited the property. She was my roommate for a while at the Arizona boarding school we both attended, and my friend for those four years. She was a cowgirl, a rodeo star; she chewed tobacco and once tried to teach me how—regrettably, since I got violently ill. Her life revolved around horses and rodeos, and the land that became my father's escape from the world was once going to be hers. When my parents first drove onto the property, they didn't know of the coincidence; but they soon did. It seemed perfect that the land changed hands the way it did.

Maybe a similar thing will happen now, I try to tell myself. I try to imagine someone else finding the memorable spots on the ranch, appreciating the scars of history left on a tree, the initials of a family painted on a rock. But my mind rebels. I keep trying, because I think I should be prepared. I can sense it even when it's unspoken.

WHEN MY MOTHER TOLD ME on the phone one afternoon that the ranch had been put up for sale and listed with Sotheby's, I felt as if the wind had been knocked out of me. When I finally could speak, I mumbled, "Well . . . I'm disappointed."

I had assumed, for some reason, that my father would be the first loss—that I would say goodbye to him, and then fight for the ranch, try somehow to keep it within the family. But the ranch is going first.

I went to the closet, took out the shirt of his that I have, and put it on, suddenly desperate to touch something that belonged to him.

On my last visit to Los Angeles, there was a moment at my parents' house which I have tried to push aside because it stirred up feelings I didn't want to have. I can't push it aside now, nor can I ignore the feelings. I needed an envelope, and I went into my father's study to get one from his desk. It was the desk that took me back. I was a young girl again, tiptoeing into my parents' bedroom when I knew they weren't there, to sit at my father's desk. I opened drawers, looked at the stack of cream-colored stationery with "Ronald Reagan" embossed across the top. I ran my hands over the paper—it was smooth, finely made. Later, when I began writing poetry, I would take some of his stationery and write poems on it. In the center drawer, he kept three-by-five-inch note cards, which were already filled with his cramped, distinctive handwriting. These were his speeches, some already given, some in the process of being written. Even as an actor, he was in demand for speaking engagements.

I would sit at his desk to know him better, to be closer to him. He was there, in the drawers, in the fine paper, the note cards, the pen set he rarely used because he preferred cheaper ballpoint pens.

Decades later, I am at the same desk, looking for an envelope, overcome by a wave of emotion. The desk will end up at the library. The wood is dark—mahogany, I think—carved along the edges. The top is leather; I used to put my face on it, breathe in the smell of the leather, feel it cool and smooth against my cheek. Now as I search for an envelope, I am also searching for a piece of his stationery—the cream-colored paper with "Ronald Reagan" across the top. It's suddenly vital that I find a piece of it. But I don't. This is the desk of a man who has not used it for a long time, and never will again. It's more of a storage bin now.

He sat here—writing, daydreaming at times. I can see him so clearly—head bent in concentration, writing in his cramped penmanship, filling up yellow pads and note cards. I can see him look up, blink his eyes, and smile at his young daughter as she comes in to ask him a question.

I wonder in how many ways I will lose my father.

He said once, "If the ranch isn't heaven, it at least has the same zip code." When he was president, he insisted on going to the ranch often, if only for a day or two. He told Mike Deaver that those visits would let him do his job better, and would help him live longer.

I escape from my father's slow dying by plunging into fantasy; I imagine bringing the ranch back to life, allowing cows and horses to once again roam the acres, getting ducks for the pond and keeping the trails clear for riding. I imagine that somewhere beyond this disease, beyond the clusters of neurons that can no longer receive or transmit information, he would know. I hold onto these images, these fantasies until I crash into reality. We have to let go of the ranch. My father will never go there again—never ride the trails or stare up at the sky and hill-sides.

"The ranch is for sale now," my mother tells us, making her sad phone call to each one of us. I hear the scrape of pain in her voice, and the way she is trying to pull herself above it, hold herself together. This is hard for her, I know, and I feel guilty for my selfishness. I don't want all these things to change! I feel like saying— screaming, even—a childish girl emerging inside me, shaking her fist at life and all its unpredictable turns.

Maureen's voice, when I call her, is shaky from crying. "Our animals are buried there," she says. "Dad built the lake, the fences."

"I know, I know," I tell her. I don't know what to do with her pain. I don't know what to do with my own.

Maureen once thought that our father could live out the last chapter of his life, the last stages of Alzheimer's, at the ranch. It made sense to her. She pictured him gazing at the green grass hills and the dome of sky. Early on, I pictured him giving me riding lessons again, just as he did when I was young. You think like this when you don't know what to expect from a disease. Alzheimer's pulls in the boundaries of the world. The endless sky and sloping hills are too much space for him now—they frighten him. And he doesn't remember the subtleties of dressage and executing a perfect jump on horseback.

We are on a pilgrimage here, leaving more things behind with each mile, having no idea what we will lose next.

M Y  M O T H E R  W A L K E D  onto the stage at the Republican convention looking so tiny, partly because my father's absence was so huge. He was there on the large screen behind her—the final image from the six-minute film which preceded her entrance. He was there in the strategy of the Republican Party—evoke the memory of Ronald Reagan, and maybe we can capture the heart of the country again. But his absence, and the sight of my mother walking out, small and alone, dressed in white, were what touched people's hearts and brought the audience to tears.

During her short speech, she also fought back tears, adding even more emotion to what seemed like an interlude in the typical convention fare. Political concerns were suspended, and people were affected by a very human drama. There was never a possibility of my attending the convention—my mother understood that; the candidate, the party platform . . . I didn't even need to explain it to her. But I would never have missed watching the tribute to my father and my mother's appearance.

I knew he was watching it also, in Los Angeles, sitting in his favorite chair. I told myself that he was smiling at the emotion being unleashed there, emotion that transcended politics—no strategist could have created it. He always appreciated the simple truth of human feelings, of relationships. As entrenched as he was in politics, he relished the moments when ideology was set aside and a bridge was formed between people. He delighted in recounting how he and Gorbachev liked each other as men and related to each other as two people who had come from humble beginnings to stand face-to-face in the spotlight of history at a crucial time. They forged a friendship; to my father, that said everything.

He and Mikhail Gorbachev met in Geneva in 1985 to discuss, among other things, SDI and future relations between the two superpowers of the world. It would not be overly dramatic to say that the fate of the world was at stake, yet he never lost sight of the smaller, human concerns. My parents had been loaned a villa on Lake Geneva. In the bedroom where they slept, there was an aquarium belonging to the children who normally occupied the house, and my father had promised to feed their goldfish. He had kept his promise, but he returned one night to find one of the fish dead. He asked someone on his staff to put the fish in a box, take it to a pet store in Geneva, and try to find one exactly like it. The staff person found two goldfish, which my father put into the aquarium, and then he wrote the children a note explaining what had happened.

EARLY ON in this campaign year, Robert Dole said, "I'll be another Ronald Reagan if you want me to be." As if this were possible. As if he could manufacture my father, put him together like a paint-by-number drawing, and then imitate him. You really don't get it, I thought, when I heard that quote. In the film that was shown at the convention, Billy Graham described my father as "the most uplifting person I've ever been around." You don't decide to be that; you don't compose it like an assignment. It's just part of you—or it's not. Ronald Reagan could reach beyond people's politics and stir their hearts, not just memorize a speech.

My mother was alone on the stage, standing in for my father, because he couldn't be there, because he will never be there again. And people wept because they missed him.

The film showed him vibrant, smiling, his eyes sparkling. When the camera panned the audience and people were crying, I thought, If you saw his eyes now you'd cry even more. His eyes used to look like summer— clear blue, sunny. But the climate in them has changed; there are more shadows, less sunlight. While my mother was in San Diego, my father said to one of the people caring for him, "My whole world is upside down now."

My mother ended her short speech by saying that my father "still sees the shining city on the hill." But it's not here, in this world. He looks past us now to things we can't see yet.

## OCTOBER 1996

There is something that happens in the death of a parent which people are reluctant to talk about—it feels blasphemous, as if the experience of bereavement were being dishonored. But if people are being very honest, or very brave, they will tell you that in the process of losing a parent to death, something within them was born— something that had been waiting beneath the surface for years, decades. No other loss, no other experience in life, can give birth to the part of ourselves that steps out of the shadows once we have whispered our last goodbye to either our mother or our father.

It has nothing to do with the nature of our relationship with that parent. In the best and the worst relationships, there is a singular truth: we are eclipsed by our parents. They are in front of us, between us and our own mortality—or so it seems—and between us and full adulthood. They define us, determine the positioning of our lives; we are the children, they are the parents. The only thing that can alter that is death.

When my mother spoke of losing her parents and said, "You realize you're nobody's little girl anymore," she was speaking of the sadness that attends that passage. But there is something else, far removed from sadness—a gentle shifting deep within the psyche that allows our true self, our adult self, to step in front of the child we used to be and take its place in the world.

It's archetypal, this confluence of death and birth; mythology is rich with it. In Maya mythology, Lady Death not only tends to the dying, but turns babies in the womb so they can be easily born and makes milk flow in a mother's breasts.

In the tarot, the death card is often representative of a birth waiting to happen, if only the passageway will open—the passageway being the death of something else.

In nature, the cycle of life to death to life is always evident. When my father showed me green shoots peeking up out of ashen ground after our ranch had burned, he was teaching his child that death is only a clearing for birth. Years later, I heard him say that the Indians used to deliberately burn acres of land that were being choked with old growth; they did it to give new life a chance. He lamented that in our modern culture, we can't do things like that. Obviously, we can't—there have to be laws against setting fires—but there is an aspect to it that's terribly sad. We've lost our ease with the cycle of life and death; we've forgotten that it is a cycle, that death allows new life to be born. In our fear of death, we have grown fearful of birth, trapped in a prison that holds little promise of escape.

But ask someone who has buried a parent what was born in them with that death, and there is an obvious relief. Someone has asked; it must be all right to acknowledge it, to admit that fresh light flooded in.

Two of my women friends recently lost their mothers. I asked each of them if beyond the grief there was new life, the feeling of being born, waking from a deep sleep—a hibernation. They both said that that was their experience. One described it as a sense of lightness in the corners of her spirit, even though she was so close to her mother that the loss itself felt leaden and huge. "I've wondered if maybe the times I feel lightest are the times when she's floating around, lifting me out of myself," she said. Who knows . . . we touch on thoughts, ideas, trying to make sense of a great and overwhelming mystery. There are always those ahead who are more schooled in grief. We who are coming up behind watch them closely.

My other friend, who is a mother herself, said that the adult in her was summoned forth only after her mother died. She finally had the courage to divorce her husband after years of a marriage that wasn't working, after years of rationalizations and excuses. When her mother died, a braver woman emerged, one willing to accept the ending of a relationship and step firmly into a new phase of her life.

Maybe it's as simple as this: the high dive of grief plunges us into the deepest waters we've ever known. We go down and down, we hold our breath, and then we come back up, bursting through the surface as people we couldn't have been without that dive. There is a Sufi prayer: "Shatter my heart so a new room can be created for a Limitless Love."

MY FATHER IS DYING gradually, as if some enormous blade is shearing off parts of him. If I hold to the idea of birth coming from death, I suppose that means my birth is a long process as well. At times I break down, cry more tears than I knew I had, and I wonder who I will be if this goes on and on. Maybe I'll drown in my own sorrow. At other times, I seem to be watching from the sweet float of remove—I'm fascinated and awestruck by the interplay between living and dying.

The other day I caught my reflection in the closet mirror as I was putting away some clothes, and I didn't recognize my own eyes. I stopped, peered into them, and thought, If I met someone with eyes like these I would think this person was far away, on an island of her own. I wondered who I was becoming, who was in there waiting to come out.

At this point, everything seems messy, confused; I'm a work in progress. And because death is ultimately the instructor, everything I have ever felt or thought about death and dying has come to the surface—out of sequence, defying chronology, as if the years I have lived were in a grab bag and someone else's hand were shuffling through it. I am a young girl, lying in her bed at night, shivering with fear at the enormous realization of death—nothingness— Where do we go? What happens? Questions no one can answer with any authority. I am nineteen, strung out on drugs, sitting in a bathroom with a razor blade . . . it would be so easy . . . the sharp edge, my soft veins. I am forty-one, sitting beside my father, thanking him for teaching me to talk to God so long ago, for giving me that anchor in my life. I don't tell him that it's the one anchor that has saved my life several times, when things looked hopeless and I wondered what point there was in going on. It's enough to thank him, to watch his eyes mist over as he says, "God always listens to us." Already, my father was retreating to a place beyond words, but he offered me those, and I took them eagerly, like the hungry child I always was.

I am all those people and none of them. I wake up each morning to eyes in the mirror that I don't yet recognize. I imagine a friend asking me someday what was born in me after going through the death of a parent; I know I'll have an answer, one that's still hiding in the shadows, that I get glimpses of, but can't yet see.

# FEBRUARY 1997, LOS ANGELES

I read recently that the air on earth recycles itself. With any inhalation, one might be breathing in the same molecules of oxygen that Geronimo once did, or Thomas Jefferson, even the dinosaurs.

I think of this as I walk through the glass doors of my father's Century City office and into the cool interior. Someday he won't be able to come in here anymore. Eventually the office will have to be moved to some smaller space and someone else will inhabit these high penthouse rooms. Whoever it is will work here, run their business, and breathe in the same air that once traveled in and out of my father's lungs. They probably won't think about it. But I do.

With Alzheimer's, patterns and structure are important. My father has been on a steady plateau for a while now and his days are predictably structured. He comes into the office for a few hours during which some visitors are allowed to spend a brief amount of time with him. They shake his hand, have pictures taken with him, and they leave. His lunch is brought to him and he eats by the windows that offer a sweeping view of the city. In the afternoon, he occasionally plays golf or goes for a walk, always accompanied by Secret Service agents who have had to learn the mysterious choreography of this disease. It's a challenge to fill the hours for him. Holidays and rainy days are particularly difficult.

He is sitting behind his desk when I walk in; I notice there is nothing on it. No work, nothing written or waiting to be signed or written upon. There is a silver water pitcher and a glass, a yellow pad with little scratch marks in ink. From someone testing out a pen? Was it him? Was he going to write something? He is just sitting there, his hands folded on top of the desk, his back straight and his eyes focused on nothing. He looks as if he is waiting for someone to tell him what he should do. My heart hurts for him.

He stands up as I walk over to him. I kiss him on the cheek. His breath smells like toothpaste. Our embrace is quick and shy—a language I've always associated with him.

"Look at all these photographs you have on the shelves," I tell him. I have seen them all before, but that's not the point. I don't want him to sit back down behind that sad, empty desk.

"Yes," he says and starts moving toward the shelves.

He points to a picture of me on my wedding day and then looks at me with his eyes twinkling the way they used to—the way they rarely do now. I take his hand—it's soft, the grip is gentle—and we walk to another part of the room. He stops in front of a picture of his mother. "There's Nelle," he tells me, and then adds, "Of course, she's dead now."

I pull a book out of the shelf, titled *The Early Films of Ronald Reagan.* "Look, Dad. Here you are—all those movies you made." He was young and handsome, with a mischievous innocence in his eyes. The camera liked him.

He stands beside me as I thumb through the book. I turn to look at him as he is looking down at the pages, and I notice the back of his neck. It reminds me suddenly of his brother who just died. I never noticed a resemblance before—not there along the slope of his neck, up into his hairline. His neck seems more curved now, thicker; it looks both old and young—so vulnerable my hand longs to touch it.

He reaches out, pointing to a photograph of him and Errol Flynn.

What moments and images will remain with me, years from now, when I think of my father? The back of his neck, soft and curved, thicker with the surrender of age? Or the light grip of his hand, agreeing to be led? Maybe the clearer images will be the more ancient ones. The days when we were both younger and I wanted so much from him in the way that daughters do. We beg for attention from fathers who don't know what to do with our neediness. My father always had a sweet reserve. It was impossible to feel angry at a man who held himself back so kindly, with such a cheerful demeanor. So I turned into a one-woman storm cloud, all drama and attitude—anything to turn his eyes in my direction. He was confused by me, troubled by my unhappiness. This man who was so comfortable in his own skin could only shake his head sadly at his daughter who frequently seemed to be in turmoil over something.

Now we have settled into a pattern of silences and

soft words. We talk about ice-skating, or photographs, or horses.

"I think I'm going to be moving back to Los Angeles soon," I tell him, when his eyes leave the book of photographs and travel around the room.

"Oh?" he says.

"My landlady is selling my apartment in New York. So, yes—I think I will move back here."

He nods and smiles in a way that tells me nothing about whether or not he's understood what I said. "Okay," he says cheerfully.

I am forty-four, standing beside my father in the sun-wash of his office, an empty desk behind us. He is old now and remembers little. But we are comfortable being silent. It took all these years, with all the fights, tears, and chilly absences to arrive at this. The air between us feels weightless, no longer heavy with dramas and upset. This is the best I can do for him now—be a calm presence beside him, an easy companion in the spaces between words.

For my mother, silence has a different resonance. My parents sit at the dinner table each night as they have for forty-five years, but there is little conversation. My father concentrates on each bite of food, as if he is marshaling everything inside him to get this one task right. My mother remembers easier nights, when talk and laughter flowed between them. The memories weigh her down.

We will all go on from here somehow, the path carved out for us by a disease that will always have the upper hand. But we will have moments, and days, maybe even years. We will find laughter sometimes, float across silences. We will know always that there are shadows crisscrossed ahead of us, but we'll try to not look at them for too long. My father lives in the moment now. The best we can do for him is to try and do the same.

JUNE 3, 2004

My mother and I sit in the den of my parents' house,
on either side of the doctor who has treated my father for
the past four years. It is midday, the sun has burned away
all the morning mist, but in this room the light is cool
and shady, filtered through trees that arch over the lawn.
The doctor's eyes are bright blue; they remind me of what
my father's eyes used to look like—years ago, before time
and illness turned them chalky and pale. A memory
streams through my mind—quickly, briefly—of another
doctor who sat in this room about six years ago and looked
at me dismissively when I said that while my father's
mind was stricken with Alzheimer's, his soul was not. I'm
glad that Dr. Shaack is here now. Because the end is close
and we will most likely share my father's last moments
with him in attendance.

Ron and Doria are in Hawaii on a long-planned vaca-
tion. We have called Ron, and he has checked in with us
the last couple of days. Should he come back early? He's
scheduled to come back at the end of the week. We don't
know what to tell him.

"There is no exact science to this," Dr. Shaack tells us
gently and then gives my mother a long, direct look. "I

can tell you that by next week, your husband will not be here. Will Ron get here in time if he keeps to his plans? I don't know. Maybe not."

I wonder how he does this—tends to the dying, consoles families, bends over people who were once vibrant and healthy and are now thin shapes beneath bedclothes.

My father's eyes have not opened for days. Before that, only one would open occasionally, and not all the way. His voice is silent now. His hands—the hands that once lifted me onto horses—are so pale they blend into the blanket. They lie thin and motionless. He takes a little fluid whenever he wakes up, but most of the time he sleeps. His breathing is irregular, and sometimes it just stops as seconds tick by. Then he gulps for air, tries to push it into himself. We watch, helpless. We are witnesses to the end of a life and even though we have known this was coming for years, it feels as if we have never considered it as a reality.

For days now, we have gathered in this den as the noon sun crawls across the sky. A sad trio trying to prepare for the end, trying to intuit and mark when it will come . . . knowing that we really can't. I want to be there; I pray that I am. Every night I dread the thought that the phone will ring in the deep, still hours and the moment will have happened. My father will be gone. What if my mother isn't there? What if she too is surprised by a knock on her bedroom door in the middle of the night? How will she live if she wasn't there for my father's last moments of life? The questions tangle themselves into the swell of grief inside me.

There is a strange thing about grief, about what it

does to your senses. People will talk about it sometimes if you give them a chance. Your senses get so clear it feels like the whole world has sharpened around you. Or maybe a little bit of you is dying too and this is how it looks from that place of calm remove.

The jacaranda trees are in bloom—explosions of purple flowers, blankets of fallen blossoms along streets and lawns. The color crawls behind my eyes. It's like I've never really seen purple before. Not like this. The jasmine vines, too—flowers so white they could have been whittled from the moon. The air is heavy with their perfume. My head swims with it. I feel it in my throat like an elixir.

If I look at my own hands, I feel like I can look straight through my skin. Other people's skin, too. The silver-haired woman at the market wearing a wedding ring but buying groceries for one. You never know what is really going on in another person's life, my father used to tell me. But sometimes you do, I wish I could say to him. We all go home to our own stories. My mother has grown so used to touching my father every day—even like this, with closed eyes and ragged breath, what will her hands do without the feel of his skin on her fingertips?

Each day, my mother and I ask the nurse to leave the room so we can talk to my father. We whisper to him that we know he has to leave, and it will be okay—we'll see him again, in a better place, where no one is sick or hurting. We tell him we love him. We tell him we know he's hanging on because he never wanted to leave first, but we know with all our hearts that he won't really be leaving. Just his body. We'll feel his soul everywhere.

We decide to tell Ron he should return early. It's as if time is pounding on each minute, letting us know another has gone by. The moon is full tonight. Will my father die when the moon is round and silvery and bright? The kind of moon that used to inspire stories when I was a child? Or will it be waning . . . like him . . . growing a little fainter every hour?

# JUNE 4, 2004

This day is the same as the previous ones. I have taken to sitting cross-legged and barefoot on my father's desk as Dr. Shaack examines him, as if I'm a bird on a perch and the distance beneath me is so vast, I'd rather cling to where I'm sitting.

Then the three of us—mother, daughter, and doctor— move into the den again to discuss the end. It's close. So close. Dr. Shaack said his phone rang in the middle of the night and he was sure it was the nurse calling him. Just a wrong number. Ron is getting in tomorrow morning before dawn. Maybe he'll be in time, I think. But then Dr. Shaack asks me if I'm coming back again this evening. Should I? I ask him. You might want to, he says, blue eyes telegraphing their message, opening up wounds inside me.

Michael and his family come and gather around the bedside in a circle, whispering to each other. I'm on my perch. I don't know what they are saying. Except for Michael, most of them haven't seen my father for years. It must be hard suddenly seeing him like this.

I come back later that evening. My mother and I stand around my father's bed with Laura, the Irish nurse who talks soothingly to him in the cadence of his ancestors. We didn't deliberately look for an Irish nurse, but I've always suspected that it was fate. My father's eyes used to sparkle at her . . . when they still opened, when they still lit up as though he was thinking of something funny. That seems like a century ago now.

We are a triangle of women around his bed, talking about the end, about death, about how it sometimes happens.

"I've heard so many stories about people having a moment of clarity before they die," I tell them. "Opening their eyes, looking around, even though before they were so ill they seemed a million miles away."

Laura smiles, nods. "My father did that," she says. "Just sort of came to right before he died, looked around at all of us."

"Do you think that might happen with my father?" It's the question I desperately want an answer to, yet I dread what I suspect the answer might be.

Laura's eyes turn downward. She has been at the bedsides of many deaths, including her own father's. "I don't think so," she tells us. "Because of the Alzheimer's. It's taken so much."

My mother and I nod slowly. Okay . . . we don't really expect, only hope. I think several times that it will happen this evening; he will go with this small circle of women around him. I imagine our voices lulling him, making it okay for him to let go. At the same time, I want him to hang on until Ron arrives at dawn. Finally, I go home. I leave my mother, knowing she won't be able to sleep. She will lie on her side of the bed, the side she still sleeps on even though my father's side has been empty for three and a half years. She will close her eyes in the dark and the awful quiet and she will pray that she is holding my father's hand as he takes his last breath.

I crawl into bed with moonlight spilling through the windows and restless dreams waiting at the gates of sleep.

Several times during the night I wake up and check the phone to make sure it's working. It is. The night is late and quiet and the dial tone in my ear tells me my father is still here. I know then that he is waiting for Ron to arrive.

## June 5, 2004

I leave home at five-thirty for the ten-minute drive to my parents' house. The streets are almost empty and thick fog brushes past the windshield. Even though we have expected the end for days, and have been surprised that it hasn't come—that he could hang on this long—everything inside me whispers, This is the day my father will die. I turn the thought over in my mind, again and again. It's nothing like I thought it would be, all these years when we have known the day would come. I should feel relief that he won't be trapped any longer inside a failing body and a mind wiped clean of memory. There must be relief somewhere inside me—for his sake—for the going home that he always believed death to be. But I can't find it beneath the huge cloud of pain that fills up every corner of my being.

Yesterday the press began chasing down rumors that the end was near for my father. After all this time, I still can't figure out where they get their information. Outside the gates of my parents' house, a lone reporter with a camera is waiting in the damp fog. I almost feel sorry for him, probably because my father would.

My brother is already there, sitting beside the hospital bed; his eyes are soft and sad. His hand is resting on our father's back—a back grown thin, the bones sharp and narrow as twigs. Ron's hand is the strong one now, large and wide and capable.

The night nurse, Nancy, is still there and will be until eight. I wonder if she will be the one who is there when the moment comes, or if Laura is meant to be present. I have always believed that it is no accident who is there when someone dies. Dr. Shaack has already been called and will be there soon. My father's breathing is even more ragged, and his closed eyes are rimmed in shadow.

This room has been the center of the house for years now, ever since my father became bedridden after falling and breaking his hip. My mother eats dinner in here. We have gotten used to gathering around this bed. But on this white gauzy morning, everything is different. Ron rarely takes his eyes off our father's face, as if he is memorizing every detail, or perhaps having a silent dialogue with him. Only a couple of months ago we were laughing about how our father still perked up at sweets. Alzheimer's stole many things, but not his love of desserts.

By eight, Dr. Shaack has been there for a while. Laura comes and Nancy, in tears, leaves. She knows she will never see my father again. So this is who will be around him, I think. We drink tea, try to eat some breakfast, talk softly and occasionally laugh affectionately at some memory of our father—the way he tried to hide his vegetables beneath mashed potatoes or rice at the dinner table; the time he discovered leaves at the ranch that, when wet, lathered like soap. "Dad thought that would be the next wave of bathing products," Ron says. We recount his unfailing humor, his way of always seeing the world in sunlight.

As the morning goes on and sun burns through the fog, his breathing grows more threadbare. At several moments we think this is it. We tighten the circle around him, touch him lightly, tell him we love him. He inhales sharply; he makes a snoring sound and we laugh through our tears . . . there is nothing else we can do. We are like shifting tides around him—moving, changing, but never leaving. The phone is ringing now. More reporters are gathering outside the gates. News reports can be heard from the television in the other room—President Reagan said to be nearing death.

It doesn't matter. All that's real is in this room.

Just before one o'clock we know that this really is it. His breathing is telling us—so shallow it sounds like it can't even be reaching his lungs. His face is angled toward my mother's. He opens his eyes—both eyes—wide. They are focused and blue. They haven't been blue like that in more than a year but they are now. My father looks straight at my mother, holds onto the sight of her face for a moment or two, and then gently closes his eyes and stops breathing.

The room is quiet except for soft weeping; my mother whispers, "That's the greatest gift you could have given me."

We had thought, the night before, that illness would define my father's last moments. He showed us how wrong we were. His soul rose above all the damage of these past years and opened his eyes so he could look with love at my mother. His eyes were blue and full and tender. It was his last act of love in this world and it was meant to cradle her until they are together again.

THE REST OF THE DAY was surreal. The helicopters came, circling the house, trying to get photos of someone, anyone. So many reporters came that the streets of Bel Air were impassable and the mortuary couldn't get through, so we told them not to try until the police could somehow corral the press behind barricades. We sat with my father's body for more than four hours and it's true what they say—the face gets smooth, unlined, as if all the ravages of life are wiped away. His room was still the center of the house. We still touched him, stroked his hand whenever we went in or out. I looked over once and saw Laura smoothing the blanket over his feet like she's done for years. There was no other room we wanted to occupy. "I don't want to leave him," my mother said.

It doesn't matter that you know the body is now empty, that the soul is free and everywhere—not locked inside flesh. It doesn't matter because your eyes still want to see that body and they don't want empty space where it once lay. Finally the mortuary was able to get through the crowded streets. By then Ron had left for the airport so he could repack and come back again the following day. Laura, my mother, and I stood with our arms around each other as my father was taken away and the room seemed suddenly empty, deserted. The hospital bed looked small without him in it. And the rest of our days without him stretched out in front of us.

There will be times when we are lifted up on the back of memories, and other times when sorrow drives us

to our knees. Especially my mother, who will have moments of wondering why he had to leave first. We will wait for him to enter our dreams. We will look for him in every breeze that drifts through every open window. We will breathe deep and wait for his whisper to stream into us—tell us secrets and make us smile. And always, always we will remember that he gave us a moment that changed everything. He opened his eyes and proved that love is stronger than disease. That moment will be the silver thread we cling to as days and nights unwind. We're not always meant to know why, my father used to say; we're meant to trust.

There is a hill in Pacific Palisades, California. A paved road is there now, and elaborate estates have claimed the uppermost acres. But it used to be just a hill— walking distance from our home when I was a child— green in winter after the rains, brown and dry in summer. It was our kite-flying hill. My father would tell this story: I was small, clinging to his hand as we walked up the trail to fly our kite. One day, when we reached the top, wind swirling around us and the sky big and endless above, I stood on my tiptoes, stretched my arm up toward all that blue, and asked him, "If I reach up really high, can I touch God?" He answered, "You don't have to reach up. God is everywhere, all the time, all around us."

I will remember that now. So many decades later—after so much life has washed beneath us, after pain and regret and coming back again but wondering if there were still doubts or if everything was recorded in my father's soul—I know now that he was also talking about himself. I don't have to stand on my tiptoes or stretch my hand to the heavens. He is here. In every breath. In every moment. He never left. Just moved on. To a place where, as he always said, there is no pain or sorrow.

## EPILOGUE

Our family went through a week of public mourning. Motorcades, and the pageantry of two funeral services, one in Washington, D.C., the other at the Reagan Library in Simi Valley. People have said to me, It must have been hard to go through that so publicly. You should know that it wasn't; it helped us. The outpouring of affection for my father, the thousands of people lining streets, turning freeways into parking lots, crowding overpasses so no cars could even get through, the sight of people weeping and holding up signs and pictures . . . all of it kept us above the waterline.

After crossing the country twice, after leaving my father to lie in state at the library and in the rotunda, after watching the solemn procession of soldiers escorting him, the hard part began on Friday evening when we left my father's casket at the library. My mother finally broke down and said, "I can't leave him here," and Ron and I tried to comfort her even though we knew there was no way to lighten her pain. We were more quiet on the long drive back than we had been all week.

My parents' house was dark and empty when we got there; the housekeepers had left earlier in the day for the service at the Library and wouldn't be back for a while.

Ron, Doria, and I quickly went through the house, turning on lights. Doria cooked scrambled eggs for my mother and Ron; we opened a bottle of wine, found fruit and cheese in the refrigerator, and the four of us sat around the kitchen table watching the coverage of the Library service.

There was something sweet and normal about it all—making a mess in the kitchen and then cleaning it up. But we knew that this was the start of a difficult journey. Now we had to live with our grief. People have told me it gets easier after the first year because you've gone through all the holidays—all the markers, like Father's Day, Christmas, a birthday—and you've survived them. We had a long year ahead of us and we knew it was starting that night.

By eleven thirty the housekeepers had returned, Doria and I had cleaned up the kitchen, and we left our mother, hoping that sleep would find her in this house that is still much too quiet.

The only way through grief is through it. There are no shortcuts, no detours. But it will help to remember the faces of strangers who stood beside highways and roads just to tell us they loved the man who died on a June morning—a man who would have been humbled and brought to tears by the overwhelming show of affection for our family. Parents came out with children and dogs, tearful women held signs saying "Our Hearts Are Broken." Firemen stood on trucks or high ladders waving American flags. There were people in wheelchairs and teenagers who weren't even alive when my father was president. Sometimes we would see a person alone, standing solemnly, often saluting. All of them drove or walked just to watch the motorcade go by. They waited hours in the hot sun, or in the cold drizzle of Washington, D.C., on Friday morning as we went to the National Cathedral.

What would my father say about all this? He would keep waving at everyone, as my mother did, even though her shoulder resting against the door told of her exhaustion. He would never see this outpouring as a credit to himself, but rather as an example of people's inherent kindness—something he never doubted. Everyone who came out to watch, and mourn, and wave knew that about him. That's why they were there.

A NOTE ON THE TYPE

The text of this book was set in Garamond No. 3. It is not a true copy of any of the designs of Claude Garamond (ca. 1480–1561), but an adaptation of his types, which set the European standard for two centuries. It probably owes as much to the designs of Jean Jannon, a Protestant printer working in Sedan in the early seventeenth century, who had worked with Garamond's romans earlier, in Paris, but who was denied their use because of Catholic censorship. Jannon's matrices came into the possession of the Imprimerie nationale, where they were thought to be by Garamond himself, and were so described when the Imprimerie revived the type in 1900. This particular version is based on an adaptation by Morris Fuller Benton.

Composed by Creative Graphics,
Allentown, Pennsylvania

Printed and bound by R. R. Donnelley and Sons,
Harrisonburg, Virginia

Designed by Iris Weinstein